AI
FOR
EDUCATORS

LEARNING STRATEGIES, TEACHER EFFICIENCIES, AND A

VISION FOR AN ARTIFICIAL INTELLIGENCE FUTURE

MATT MILLER
AUTHOR OF DITCH THAT TEXTBOOK

Special discounts are available on quantity purchases by schools, school districts, associations, and others. Email books@daveburgessconsulting.com for pricing and details.

Published by Ditch That Textbook, whose printing operation is a division of Dave Burgess Consulting, Inc.

DitchThatTextbook.com
DaveBurgessConsulting.com

Book design by Najdan Mancic, Iskon Design Inc.
Proofreading by Mairead Hurley
Icons used with permission via The Noun Project

Library of Congress Control Number: 2023933910
Paperback ISBN: 978-1-956306-47-7
Ebook ISBN: 978-1-956306-48-4

First printing: March 2023

*To the forward-thinking teachers
who use their "tomorrow glasses"
to do everything in their power
to prepare students for their
future, not our present.*

*Thank you for your hard work
and open-mindedness.*

Contents

ACKNOWLEDGEMENTS

Thank you to Holly Clark and Ken Shelton, my co-presenters and thought partners, for your bravery to step up to a new topic and share about it when few did.

Thank you to Karly Moura and Jeff Miller, my teammates at Ditch That Textbook, for encouraging me, providing insight and feedback, and working tirelessly with me to support educators all over the world.

Thank you to my wife, Melanie; my children, Cassie, Hallie, and Joel; my mom, Jacki; and my dad, Jeff. Your love and support mean the world to me. You've always stood beside me and encouraged me to pursue my dreams.

Thanks to friends, acquaintances, and colleagues who have pushed my thinking about artificial intelligence and its place in education, including but not limited to: Donnie Piercey, Jen Giffen, Jamie Gladfelter, and Jens Seip.

A HUGE thank you to the subscribers of the Ditch That Textbook email newsletter and my followers on social media. You've generously shared your thoughts, concerns, and ideas through your replies, participation in surveys, and personal communication. Your perspective is invaluable.

And finally, I'm thankful to my Lord and Savior Jesus Christ, the author of my faith and the provider of all good things in my life.

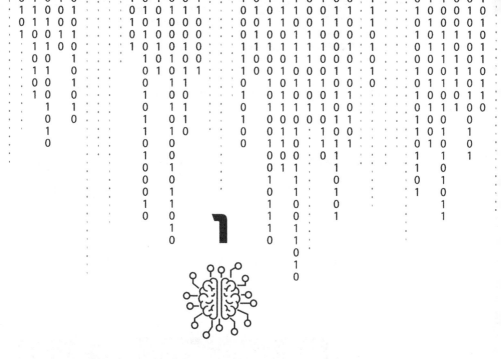

WELCOME TO THE
AI REVOLUTION

When you hear the term "artificial intelligence," what comes to mind?

It might conjure images right out of a dystopian novel, bots taking over the world and dominating humans.

If you're of a certain age, you might think of Rosey the Robot from the cartoon series, *The Jetsons*, or even HAL 9000, the AI computer from the movie *2001: A Space Odyssey*.

You might think of robotic arms in a factory.

Or the AI waiters at Cafe 80s in the movie *Back to the Future Part II.*

For a while, AI was a thing of the future. Even though it was making its way into our everyday lives, we didn't always notice it.

At least, I didn't. Not until it stormed onto the scene in 2022 and demanded my attention.

"THIS THING WRITES FUNNY STORIES!"

I was dropping my kids off at our church for youth group on Friday, December 9, 2022. We hustled in from the cold parking lot, through the double entry doors, and into the big dining hall where everyone socialized.

Suddenly, we were met by a group of enthusiastic middle schoolers.

"Hey, have you guys seen this thing? It's called ChatGPT, and it can write these hilarious stories!"

We peered at one of their phones, which was displaying text about something like a dinosaur and Harry Styles preventing a zombie apocalypse and saving the world.

"Ha! That is hilarious!" I said.

I promptly became a user of ChatGPT, a creation by OpenAI that lets humans interact with its artificial intelligence in a conversational way.

I thought I was an early adopter. I was wrong.

ChatGPT amassed more than 1 million users in five days (Brockman, 2022). *Five days.* More than 1 million users beat me to ChatGPT, and I learned about it just a week after it was released publicly.

It took Instagram about two months to reach 1 million users. Spotify took five months.

After that, ChatGPT sprinted to 100 million monthly active users in two months (Hu, 2023).

One million users in five days. One hundred million users in two months.

How did ChatGPT take off so quickly?

SCIENCE FICTION TURNED REALITY

ChatGPT is an artificial intelligence assistant created by OpenAI. Users provide it with questions or prompts, and ChatGPT responds. It answers by drawing from an enormous dataset. It uses natural language processing so it responds and interacts in language that feels human.

ChatGPT was a friendly face on AI, something many of us knew about through science fiction novels and movies. It was the public's first real, official face-to-face interaction with artificial intelligence. Sure, AI has already been a part of our lives. Amazon had been suggesting products to us for a while. Our phones could unlock themselves with a face. And the algorithm for Facebook, Twitter, and TikTok controlled what posts we saw.

But this...this was a conversation with AI. And it seemed so, so *human*.

Pretty quickly, we all started to realize what it was capable of. On social media, you started seeing people use it to:

► Write rap song lyrics about asparagus and other vegetables.
► Gather recipes for the week and create a shopping list for the grocery store.
► Create code in a variety of programming languages— code that worked!
► Write poetry in the style of poets that had been dead for centuries.
► Explain existentialism in terms a child can understand.
► Brainstorm party themes for a 29-year-old.

For us educators, the gears in our brains started turning pretty quickly.

"Wait," we thought. "If it can do all of that, what's stopping it from writing our students' essays and completing their homework for them?"

"What does this change in education?"

STUDENTS, MEET THE AI WORLD

In short, AI is going to change a lot in the education world.

Wait. Let's not be shortsighted. AI will change *the world* in some ways.

AI expert Kai-Fu Lee writes, "Artificial intelligence (AI) could be the most transformative technology in the history of mankind—and we may not even see much of this sweeping change coming. That's because we often overestimate what technologies can do in five years, and underestimate what they will be able to do in 20" (2022).

If AI is going to change the world in the near future, we need to prepare students for that world. That means we'll need to change too.

Here's one big change we'll need to make:

One of the first reactions so many of us had to the release of ChatGPT was: "Are there AI detectors? Can I find out if this writing is done by my students or artificial intelligence? Can we block it?"

For our students' sake, to prepare them for the future, we can't look at the world through "today glasses." We must use our "tomorrow glasses."

That's looking at the situation through "today glasses."

"Today glasses" judge AI (and other innovations and technology) based on the reality of today. The norms and expectations of today. Our view today of what's important, what's ethical, what's relevant.

For our students' sake, to prepare them for the future, we can't look at the world through "today glasses."

We must use our "tomorrow glasses."

Think of a student who's 10 years old today. In eight years, she will graduate high school. In another four years, she will graduate college. She'll enter the workforce in 12 years. At that point, artificial intelligence will be 12 years more sophisticated than it is right now.

Don't forget what Kai-Fu Lee just told us. We *overestimate* what technologies can do in five years. We *underestimate* what they will be able to do in 20.

What does this mean for that 10-year-old student? How can we prepare students for that future world?

And what does that look like in the classroom today? How can our day-to-day lessons support students in light of that future?

TEACHERS, MEET THE AI WORLD

As educators, we're hard-wired to want what's best for our students. It's our natural tendency to think about how to support them and what they need. We just did that above.

But let's stop for a moment and think about ourselves.

What does AI have in store for us? Will it render teachers obsolete?

No way. I mean, who would help kindergarteners tie their shoes and open their milk cartons? Who would watch middle schoolers' eyes light up reading a book—and suggest a similar one to them? Who would beam when high schoolers talk about their future—and tell them why they're convinced it will work based on what they've seen in the classroom?

Certain parts of learning can be supported by technology and artificial intelligence. The essence of a teacher is brains, heart, and humanity.

I believe we're always going to need that.

I also believe AI is going to give us the most precious, most valuable, most sought-after resource for educators...the one that teachers never have

AI won't change everything. But it will change a lot.

enough of, the one that would empower them to realize their classroom dreams if they just had a little more.

Time. AI is going to give us time.

It's also going to change the kinds of assignments we give and how we provide feedback on them.

That's just scratching the surface.

AI won't change everything. But it will change a lot.

LET'S MAKE SENSE OF AI IN THE CLASSROOM

The purpose of this book is to help educators understand artificial intelligence and how it might impact education.

You'll see how AI's presence will impact classrooms in the short term—and how it may change what we do in classrooms long term. You'll get perspective on hot topics like cheating and plagiarism, ethical implications, and preparing students for a future with AI. At the end of each chapter, I'll include a key definition so you can learn the basics of AI.

This book is also a snapshot in time. It was published in the spring of 2023. At that time, the world was still buzzing about ChatGPT by OpenAI. It wondered about its integration with Microsoft tools. It was learning about Google's AI chatbot, Bard.

The examples, products, and technology mentioned in this book will become out of date quickly. (It's hard enough to keep the chatbot details up to date before publishing the book!) Thankfully, the book's focus isn't the newest and latest AI product details.

The book focuses on classroom implementation. It's practical. It helps you understand the general concepts and how they will apply to day-to-day learning in the classroom. It also better positions you to help your students thrive in the world and workforce they'll one day enter.

By the way, this book was written by a human. It's written by me. I'll consult a variety of resources, including the internet and some AI tools. At the end of each chapter, I'll be transparent about how much I think I created as a human and how much I created with artificial intelligence. I hope that transparency will model how the technology can be used. I also hope it will show that human intellect and creativity, aided by artificial intelligence, can create something helpful and unique.

Also, for context: I studied journalism, Spanish, and political science in college. I didn't study computer science. But for our work in education, we don't need intricate knowledge of how AI works. We need the basics, but most importantly, we need to know how to implement it effectively and responsibly. That, thankfully, is right in my wheelhouse. If you're familiar with all the free teacher resources I create at Ditch That Textbook (DitchThatTextbook.com), you'll feel right at home with this book.

The use of AI in our world is changing quickly. ChatGPT will be the most rudimentary generative AI chatbot our students will ever encounter. It's like the MySpace of AI chatbots. We'll look back on it and chuckle at how powerful we thought it was.

Let's wrap our brains around this so we can help our students—and ourselves!—thrive with this technology.:

KEY DEFINITION

ARTIFICIAL INTELLIGENCE (AI)

The ability of a computer or machine to do things that would normally require human intelligence. AI involves training a computer to "think" like a human. When humans think, they often follow certain patterns and draw from their memories. For example:

- ► Our future decisions are informed by past decisions.
- ► We weigh possible options and choose a scenario that's most likely to be successful.
- ► We rank and sort based on our own priorities.
- ► We choose words and phrases that best suit our intended outcome.

Machines can be trained to do that. We can apply that artificial intelligence in a variety of areas to do things that only humans used to do. For example:

- ► AI-operated robots can do tasks that used to require human hands, eyes, and brains.
- ► AI can be trained to communicate in language that feels natural to us.
- ► AI can recognize things in images and videos that only humans could before.

Bot Check: 90% human created, 10% artificial intelligence created.

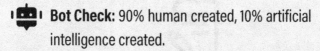 **Used AI to:** Identify where AI exists in our daily lives, create a definition of AI.

Find bonus resources, shareable infographics, and more at:
AIforEDUbook.com

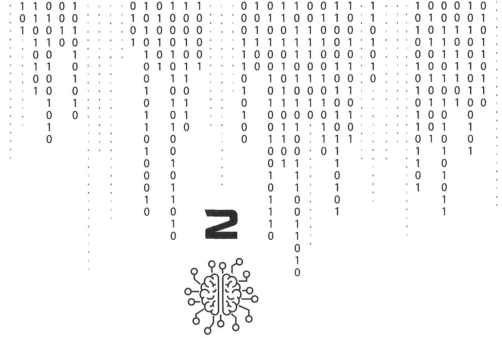

IMAGINING THE AI-INTEGRATED CLASSROOM

GRASPING THE REAL IMPACT ON EDUCATION THROUGH THE GROWTH OF AI

Futurists and education thought leaders have talked about the impact of artificial intelligence on education for years.

But the genie was let out of the lamp, so to speak, with the release of ChatGPT.

As people started to use it and understand what it could do, the questions began:

- ► Students asked: "Wait, can this write my English essays for me? And do my math homework?"
- ► Teachers asked: "How will I run class when students can ask a chatbot to do everything for them?"
- ► IT staff asked: "Can we block this? If we do, will it really change anything?"

The more that AI becomes assimilated into our day-to-day lives, the more that it'll impact the classroom.

What impact will the spread of generative AI have on classrooms, schools, and school districts?

Here are some implications I believe it will have.

STUDENTS CAN USE GENERATIVE AI TOOLS (LIKE CHATGPT) TO DO THEIR ASSIGNMENTS.

There. We're all thinking about it. I'll just say it clearly and plainly. Students can use it to do their work. They can. They will. This includes lots of assignment types, like essays, research reports, speech scripts, written summaries, and more. Students can type a prompt into the AI chatbot—the prompt you gave them or something else that'll generate the result they need. And they can copy and paste the work into a document or your learning management and submit it. They can do it.

TURNITIN AND OTHER PLAGIARISM CHECKERS CAN'T RELIABLY CATCH IT.

These plagiarism checkers, in the pre-ChatGPT world, checked student work against previously-submitted student work, other academic content, and internet searches. If they found significant matches, they flagged the work as plagiarized. Using those methods, plagiarism checkers wouldn't be able to detect content created by generative AI tools like ChatGPT. That's because these AI tools do original work every time. They aren't copying human-created work. They're writing it spontaneously. TurnItIn could try to check the AI-created work against its database, but because it isn't copied from another source, it's unlikely to flag it as plagiarism.

As of the publication of this book, plagiarism checker tools are undoubtedly scrambling to incorporate some form of AI detector into their systems. We will discuss the concepts of cheating and plagiarism in the AI-integrated world in a later chapter.

AS EDUCATORS AND HUMANS, WE MUST ADDRESS CONCERNS.

Ever since artificial intelligence was created, we've seen the warning signs. With all the possibilities AI brings globally and to education, we must tread carefully.

There are biases built into AI models and datasets. Those datasets have gaps and voids. AI tools make mistakes—mistakes that can potentially create misunderstandings in our students' views of the world that might not be corrected.

The existence of AI also brings up tons of ethical questions. What jobs will be outsourced to AI, becoming irrelevant? What damage will be done to certain communities and careers, including the creative fields? Based on access, cost, and other factors, will it create further inequities based on income, location, race, and gender?

I'm still optimistic. You'll see that in the pages of this book. But we can't fly haphazardly into this new frontier without keeping an eye on its threats and challenges. We'll address these in a future chapter.

AI TOOLS WILL CAUSE US TO RETHINK TRADITIONAL ASSIGNMENTS.

Essays. The student-written essay has taken the spotlight since these language-generation AI tools have emerged. Everyone seems to be talking about the implications of AI on essays as classwork. Articles in *The Atlantic* proclaimed "The College Essay is Dead" (Marche, 2022) and "The End of High-School English" (Herman, 2022).

Again, these opinions look at the world through today glasses. They're based on how we see the world right now, with the criteria we use right now to judge. Who can blame teachers for doing that—looking at their classes through today glasses? They're the ones who have to teach class today. And tomorrow. And the next day. And next week. AI is here, and they're in classrooms figuring out how teaching and learning move forward.

These generative AI tools force us to ask ourselves more fundamental questions. Let's use the essay as an example of how we'll need to re-evaluate what we do in the classroom.

1. **Why have we used essays as evaluative tools?** Essays have allowed teachers to see how students think. To understand their processes. To help them explore a line of thought. To encourage them to recall new material and strengthen it in their long-term memories.

2. **Have there always been limitations to using essays as evaluative tools for learning?** Yes. One: to write a successful essay, you have to be adept at both the skill of writing and the understanding of content. Students who struggle with writing are at a disadvantage. If essays help teachers gauge student understanding of content, the writing stands in the way of that. Two: accessibility. Students who struggle physically to write with a pencil or type with

a keyboard must fight through a barrier that other students don't have. If the goal is to know how well a student understands a concept, essays present lots of prerequisites before students can even begin demonstrating understanding.

3. **Can we find other ways—better ways even—to evaluate students?** Definitely. Some alternatives include verbal responses, creative demonstrations of learning, collaborative learning, class discussions, and more. (We'll go deeper into these and others in a future chapter.)

> **We need to know our "why" to find our way.**

4. **Will these alternatives also encourage students to think on their own?** Yes. It's much harder for students to copy and paste responses mindlessly from AI tools when they're asked to do these deeper, collaborative, creative tasks. Plus, they're more authentic to the work students will do later in their lives.

To find answers going forward, we need to go back to the fundamentals, to the foundational reasons we ask students to do academic work.

We need to know our "why" to find our way.

IT'S GOING TO BE HARD BEFORE IT GETS EASIER.

There's a model that could predict how we'll feel as we learn about AI and integrate it into learning.

It's called the Gartner Hype Cycle.

According to Gartner, a tech research firm, the Hype Cycle is "a graphical depiction of a common pattern that arises with each new technology or other innovation" (2022). It shows how new technology matures, is adopted, and is applied. It wasn't made for us in education, but it can help us to see how AI may assimilate into schools.

The Gartner Hype Cycle

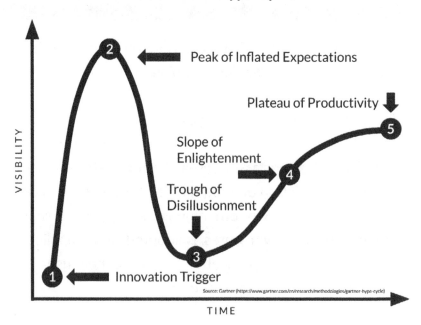

Source: Gartner (https://www.gartner.com/en/research/methodologies/gartner-hype-cycle)

► **Innovation Trigger:** In a short amount of time, there's lots of buzz. Interest spikes even though the clear, lasting uses of it are unclear.

► **Peak of Inflated Expectations:** Early successes cause expectations to soar. It's gone viral and has everyone's attention, even though its implementation isn't widespread.

► **Trough of Disillusionment:** The expectation bubble pops. Frustrations and failures cause many to drop out. Slow improvements keep early adopters going.

► **Slope of Enlightenment:** The benefits become more understood. The uses are more practical. Buy-in grows as the technology matures.

► **Plateau of Productivity:** It's going mainstream. It still hasn't lived up to the early inflated expectations, but its use is really paying off now.

If that's how the adoption of a new technology is seen by investors, how could this apply to us? How could we similarly see the implementation of AI in schools?

Here's my interpretation of the Gartner Hype Cycle for educators:

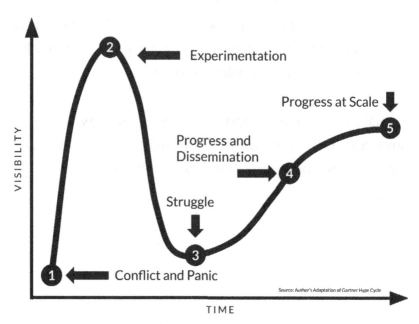

Educator & AI Hype Cycle

Source: Author's Adaptation of Gartner Hype Cycle

► **Conflict and Panic:** "What is this new AI stuff? I don't like it. It feels like cheating."

► **Experimentation:** "Oh wow, these AI tools can do some cool stuff. It's a neat trick, but it's probably just a fad. I'm still not ready to use it."

► **Struggle:** "These AI tools have lots of flaws. I have concerns. They aren't custom-created to do what I do, and they're hard to implement. It's just too much work. I'm giving up."

► **Progress and Dissemination:** "I'm reading online about teachers who are using these AI tools to save time and do really interesting learning work in class. Now that others are sharing what works for them, I can see it. I'm willing to use it in limited ways.

► **Progress at Scale:** "Some of these AI tools are in my learning management system and my favorite apps. I've learned how they work. They can save me time and improve learning in my classroom. I get it. This is going to work."

How do we get to "Progress at Scale"? The key, I think, will be what makes the teacher community great. We freely share what works in our classrooms. We tell the teacher next door, the friend on social media, and anyone who will listen at teacher conferences and online. Then, when we learn what works from someone else, we share the idea with others until it grows exponentially.

Let's be patient. Take small steps. Be willing to learn from shortfalls. Play the long game. And share freely.

In the end, we're in this together. The whole community of educators will support each other, and we'll find ways to thrive.

SCHOOL AND CLASS USES OF ARTIFICIAL INTELLIGENCE AREN'T ALL BAD.

If the first items in this list have made you feel a bit hopeless, here's where the sunshine starts to peek through the clouds. Early news reports focused almost exclusively on the cheating connection between these AI tools and schools. But these AI tools weren't created to be cheating tools for students. They're built to answer questions, gather information, and help us complete tasks.

Artificial intelligence in the hands of students and teachers will, in many ways, help us to focus on what's most important and save us time.

- ► They will help teachers create differentiated learning materials to support students right where they are.

- ► They will provide a first line of feedback for students before requiring the teacher's attention.

- ► They will provide individualized learning and "just in time" learning at a scale that a flock of teachers couldn't in a classroom.

AI will help us scale up the essence of what makes us teachers to bigger and broader levels. Instead of spending so much time on menial, trivial tasks, we'll be able to dedicate more of that time to what matters most.

> **WE'VE BEEN HERE BEFORE. AND WE'VE EMERGED FROM IT BETTER.**

The only constant in education, it seems, is change. Sometimes innovations come and go. Sometimes they stay. In the end, we keep what works and what supports good teaching and learning.

Some examples from the not-too-distant past and some recent examples:

CALCULATORS

- ▶ **The fears:** Teachers worried that these machines would make students worse at math because they couldn't do calculations by hand. (A teacher saying that didn't age well: "You need to know how to do this because you won't always have a calculator in your pocket.")

- ▶ **What happened?** Calculators saved us from doing routine calculations so students could grasp more complex concepts, helping them progress to advanced math more quickly.

SEARCH ENGINES

► **The fears:** When students got access to computers with search engines, teachers worried that the ability to look up all of the answers would be catastrophic to learning.

► **What happened?** Now, we have begun focusing more on the application of those basic facts instead of just recalling them from memory.

WIKIPEDIA

► **The fears:** Because anyone could edit it, teachers worried information on Wikipedia would be inaccurate and could be manipulated by bad actors.

► **What happened?** A dedicated base of volunteer user editors keep a keen eye on Wikipedia changes, so it stays accurate. It's nimble, with precise updates often happening within minutes.

PHOTOMATH

► **The fears:** Photomath lets users input a complex math problem to see a detailed solution in seconds. Teachers worried it would nullify math homework.

▶ **What happened?** The focus shifted to showing an understanding of the process. It's a lot like giving the answers to just odd-numbered questions in the back of the textbook. Checking against the correct answers helps students know what they're doing right and wrong.

CHESS

▶ **The fears:** Because AI chess bots were so good at chess, some in the chess community worried that chess was ruined. It will destroy the experience for humans, they said.

▶ **What happened?** Instead, chess engines have improved the level of gameplay of human chess players as a whole. New strategies have been developed, too, that previously weren't widely accepted.

What are the implications of artificial intelligence on schools and education? Much like previous innovations, it will help our practice—and what our students can do—to rise like the tide. We will learn what it can do and how it can improve our lives. And like the tide when it comes in, it will cause all ships to rise.

KEY DEFINITION

GENERATIVE AI

Generative artificial intelligence (AI) is a class of AI that will generate, or create, new and original data. It can make images, videos, music, text, and more, all without the aid of a human. Generative AI models understand patterns and relationships that they identify in the tons and tons of data they analyze in their datasets. True to the word "generative," it generates new work every time it fulfills a request. There isn't a pre-written, copy-and-paste response it provides to certain questions. It interprets the request, analyzes data, and creates a new response each time.

 Bot Check: 85% human created, 15% artificial intelligence created.

 Used AI to: Write a definition of generative AI, suggest general ways that AI might change education that I could elaborate on.

Find bonus resources, shareable infographics, and more at:
AIforEDUbook.com

SHIFTING TO ACCOMMODATE A WORLD WITH AI

Conversations about how artificial intelligence will change the world will spin for years and years.

Educators will talk about how learning will look in a classroom with access to AI tools. They'll talk about the future, what part AI will play, and how to teach students so they're prepared for that future.

But there's a bigger concern in the minds of many teachers—especially those that are in the classroom right now: What should I do today?

► Now that I know what some of these AI tools can do, how do I adjust my lesson plans right away?
► How can I make sure my assignment on Tuesday challenges my students to think and develop skills, not just copy/paste from a chatbot?
► What steps can I take if I just need to teach right now and don't have time to reinvent education and earn a master's degree in AI-focused computer science?

This is a completely natural line of thought, by the way.

Don't worry about the big-picture "What's the future of education?" discussions right now if you just don't have time for them. There are plenty of pundits and talking heads to debate that on your behalf. (I dabble in that occasionally, too. I mean, hey...I'm writing this book, right?)

But you have lesson plans to write. You can't erase these AI tools. And you want the best for your students.

If you feel powerless, that's understandable.

In the next chapter, we'll look at how to plan instruction and learning with artificial intelligence integrated into your lessons. But let's take a more immediate approach here.

Let's look at some small shifts you can make right away to preserve student thinking and growth.

Consider this your "break glass in case of emergency" chapter.

PAPER AND PENCIL IS A STOP-GAP WITH LOTS OF CONCERNS.

This is a solution many educators saw when generative AI tools like ChatGPT became available, especially for writing activities. The rationale: "If students do their work on paper and pencil, then I'll know they're doing the thinking and not an AI chatbot."

I see where you're coming from. I think I see your heart in thinking this way. You're thinking that this preserves the kinds of learning activities you've done before—activities that have gotten you and your students the results that you want! By thinking this way, you might perceive these AI tools as a threat to what has worked for you before, and this paper and pencil option seems to eliminate that threat.

If you want to go this route, consider some of the concerns that go with it:

1. **Paper and pencil can create more barriers to demon-strating understanding than it removes.** Technology provides students with lots of accessibility tools,

like voice typing, screen readers, magnification, and translation services. It supports students with a variety of learning disabilities. Removing access to these supports can exacerbate problems for these students, who are likely already marginalized.

2. **Resourceful students can still find ways to access the tools you're trying to avoid.** They'll access the internet and AI tools on their phones under their desks (or in a restroom stall). They'll text their friends. As long as teachers have discouraged students from things they deem "cheating," students have been finding ways to use them.

3. **Paper and pencil slow down the feedback loop.** Digital work lets students work and submit from anywhere. It gives teachers instant access—even while the student is still working—to provide immediate feedback. Paper work means students have to turn it in in-person and wait to receive it back in-person to get feedback.

4. **It's not very authentic to their future.** This is an activity seen through today glasses. Blocking out the internet and these growing AI tools isn't the kind of work they'll do when they reach the workforce. It's not the kind of work we do as adults, either.

Despite all of this, if you choose to use this option, please... please, please, please...please do not plan for the long-term like this. This AI technology isn't going away, and its effects will be sprawling and widespread. We want to prepare students for their future—through tomorrow glasses—instead of preparing them for today.

MAKE USE OF CLASSROOM DISCUSSIONS.

When Google Translate started growing, people asked, "Do I need to learn a language? If a translator app can do the work, can I spend my time and effort elsewhere?" As a world language teacher, I had an existential crisis, wondering if my job was becoming obsolete.

Then, we learned, if we want to have a true conversation with another human and build relationships, we can't do that effectively by typing everything into Translate—even though *90 Day Fiancé* tried to prove otherwise.

When students discuss, they do so from their own working and long-term memory. Sure, they can look up quick answers with a search engine. They can even ask chatbots questions. But to carry on a conversation, most of the work comes from their own thinking.

Conversation is a timeless skill. We're still going to need to be able to talk to other humans and interact extemporaneously. We'll still create and support opinions. We'll still come up with questions. Even though we'll ask machines for answers sometimes, we will always want to ask humans those questions, too.

After a discussion in class, students can recap the discussion and share their reflections about it, which is much harder to do with a bot.

In response to the growth of generative AI tools, consider expanding the use of discussions in your classroom—paired discussions, small group discussions, whole-class discussions, and even asynchronous forum-style discussions.

Sure, discussions can be hard to grade. But we're not using them to assess students. We're using them to help students make meaning. To use new knowledge and ideas extemporaneously. To take them out of the package and play with them, molding them like clay to see what they can and can't make.

Students can discuss the content itself—what makes sense and what doesn't. They can compare and contrast. They can see how it transfers to other content areas. They can even reflect on what they've learned and their own learning process.

These discussions are valuable—and the thinking is done by students and not an AI chatbot.

EMBRACE COLLABORATIVE LEARNING.

Collaborative learning can have similar benefits to classroom discussions. When students work together, they're still talking about what they found, what they learned, if it fits, how to organize it, and how to communicate it effectively. Those important conversations are happening even if they're pulling information from Google, Wikipedia, or AI tools like ChatGPT.

In fact, you could argue that this is the kind of work they'll be expected to do when they enter the workforce. They're just getting practice with it today.

I caught a glimpse into the importance of this kind of work in today's workforce. I moderated a virtual panel discussion that included Victoria Thompson, a former classroom teacher who works as an education executive for Microsoft (Miller, 2023). Tech companies have become increasingly collaborative in their work, which can serve as a model of what students will be expected to do when they reach the workforce.

I asked Victoria how often she was asked if her work was being done independently, alone, by herself—in the same kind of way that we've asked students to work independently in the classroom for so many years. Here's her response:

That's a good question. Now that I think about it, there has never been a moment where they asked me if I've done something completely by myself.

Collaborative work is the future of career readiness.

A lot of what we do, quite frankly, is directly tied to not only how we support others but also how we help others, too. That's been really not only liberating for me as a working adult but also really inspiring.

I think we've all been in situations where we feel really ly siloed, and we're not encouraged to seek things out because it might be seen as a sign of weakness[...]In my role in particular and also across Microsoft, I know in my evaluations, some of my questions are directly tied to what I did to support other people, what kind of resources I utilized, how I went to places for help.

I think that ties directly into this because that's the future of career readiness.

Collaborative work is the future of career readiness. Working together to reach a shared goal is what Victoria does at Microsoft. There's a good chance many of your students will need to be skillful at that in future roles as adults—and even before they enter the workforce.

HAVE STUDENTS MAKE CREATIVE DEMONSTRATIONS OF LEARNING.

For years, teachers have leaned on the same strategy to have students show what they've learned.

Write it in a document. Write it on a sheet of paper. Turn it in.

It's efficient, but it also reduces learning to a set of facts— and also doesn't put information in context.

Let's provide creative, authentic ways for students to show what they know. Creativity in learning can help students with motivation. It can help them make use of their own unique talents and skills. It can help them feel seen and heard and noticed.

Plus, when they make something creative with what they've learned, it's much harder to copy/paste an AI chatbot's answer without doing any of the cognitive work themselves.

Creative demonstrations of learning are also very brain-friendly. When students take what they've learned—or information they've found from other sources—and create with it, they're engaging in elaboration. And that's a good thing. "Elaboration in learning involves meaning-enhancing additions, constructions, or generations that improve one's memory for what is being learned" (Levin, 1988).

> **Take what you've learned. Organize it. Make something with it. And while you do that, you're understanding better what you have.**

What does that look like? It all depends on your students, your content, and your goals.

Have you asked students to do the "type what you remember in a document" activity? Instead, students could...

► Record it in a **video**, reporting it as if they were a news anchor on the nightly news.
► Display it visually in an **infographic** with icons and snippets of text.
► Create a **storyboard** for a video in the way a YouTuber would.
► Snap pictures with their webcam to display learning in the style of **Instagram Stories.**
► Create a simple **webpage** with images, text, and videos.
► Record a **public service announcement**-style video.
► Design a **billboard** to capture the essence of the new concept.

That's just scratching the surface! In fact, this is the kind of teaching we've been writing about at Ditch That Textbook for years. You can find more creative ways for students to show what they know at DitchThatTextbook.com. While you're there, sign up for our email newsletter to get a pipeline of new teaching ideas to try in your inbox.

Take what you've learned. Organize it. Make something with it. And while you do that, you're understanding better what you have.

USE RETRIEVAL PRACTICE, BRAIN DUMPS, AND OTHER MEMORY STRATEGIES.

Retrieval practice is strengthening your long-term memory by recalling everything you can about a specific topic. It seems too easy and too good to be true, but it's been backed by cognitive science for decades. This is a study strategy that helps students strengthen what they've already learned and reflect on what they are learning.

Students can do a "brain dump," where they recall (on paper, verbally, in a document, etc.) everything they know about topics like:

- ► What do you remember from class yesterday?
- ► What do you remember about (this topic) we studied a week ago?
- ► What do you remember about (this topic) we studied last semester?
- ► What do you know about (this topic) we haven't studied yet?
- ► What do you know about (this person)?
- ► What do you know about (this very broad topic)?
- ► What do you know about (this narrow subtopic)?

Brain science (much of which can be found at RetrievalPractice.org, along with more practical teaching ideas) tells us that these brain dumps build long-term memory the best when they are ungraded. They're a study skill, not a formative assessment.

These memory strategies focus on what students have already learned, and they're pulled from student memory—not from an AI bot.

WE'RE HUMAN, AND THAT'S GOOD

We keep talking about the enormous dataset that many artificial intelligence tools have at their disposal. Thankfully, we have a huge dataset, too, and we can access it even faster than AI.

It's called the human brain.

We're not talking high-tech here. We're talking low-tech.

We don't have to train our brains the way we do with AI because we've been doing it our whole lives. We also don't have to interpret the results our brains give us.

Our brains are incredible supercomputers. They're pre-loaded with our entire life's experiences and everything we know about our students. Our brains interpret them instantly in real time. Thankfully, we will always have these supercomputers to help us process all of that.

Plus, more good news: Our brains are wireless. Their carbon emissions are minimal. Sadly, though, we do have to charge them for about eight hours every night, or they start to malfunction!

One of our greatest strengths as humans is our brains. They'll help us adjust for class tomorrow. They'll help us figure out where all of this is headed. And, using all of our teaching and life experience, they'll help us adjust to fit our students' needs.

We're perfectly positioned for this work. We've got this.

KEY DEFINITION

GPT (GENERATIVE PRETRAINED TRANSFORMER)

A type of artificial intelligence that interacts with the user in natural, understandable language. Lots of AI assistants, including ChatGPT, are powered by GPT. It's *generative* because it creates a new response every time. It's *pretrained* because it has learned from a massive dataset. And it's a *transformer* because it transforms its results into language that feels natural to the user. New versions of GPT are constantly being developed. Each new GPT version becomes more powerful, allowing it to do more and interact in more natural ways.

 Bot Check: 85% human created, 15% artificial intelligence created.

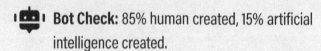 **Used AI to:** Write a definition of GPT, suggest ideas I could elaborate on regarding immediate classroom shifts in light of AI.

Find bonus resources, shareable infographics, and more at:
AIforEDUbook.com

30 WAYS AI CAN SUPPORT TEACHING AND LEARNING

USING AI TOOLS TO FACILITATE MEANINGFUL TEACHING AND LEARNING

A s artificial intelligence tools have developed, we've had so many questions. Is this good? Can AI be harmful? What is the source of its responses?

Will robots take over the world? (And if they do, will they be fans of coffee or tea? Dogs or cats? Coke or Pepsi? I mean, we need answers. Inquiring minds want to know!)

One question seems to stand above them all with educators, though.

Can we use this to teach and learn authentically? And if so, how?

My answer is: ABSOLUTELY. We can use it.

Thankfully, the education community is amazing at providing the "how." As I mentioned earlier, we're so good at trying things, finding what works and what doesn't, and sharing it with others. We will figure this out together, even though it will take some time.

Here are 30 ideas for using AI assistants in classrooms, brainstormed by me (a human), by other humans (with credit provided), and by the AI bots (because why not ask them, too?).

1. USE AI AS A DEEPER SOURCE OF INFORMATION THAN GOOGLE.

Results on search engines are limited to the web pages they index. Many times, they lack nuance and depth. We can ask AI assistants to provide us the information we need to drive a class conversation forward. Do it before class starts to pre-load your instruction with content. Do it during one-on-one conversations with students for "just in time" information. Do it during whole-class discussions to model how AI can support our learning. The bot's response isn't the first and last word in the conversation. Rather, it just provides details that we can use to discuss a topic.

PROMPT TIP: Use follow-up questions to probe for full answers to questions.

2. USE AI FOR LOTS OF GOOD EXAMPLES.

Think about how musicians and artists develop their styles. They copy their mentors. Musicians emulate other musicians they see as influential. Artists often take blank canvases to galleries or parks and paint what they see. Fashion designer Yohji Yamamoto once said, "Start copying what you love. Copy copy copy copy. At the end of the copy, you will find yourself."

This is also the benefit of being well-read. When students see enough good examples, they start to know what to expect from good writing. Good reasoning. Good logic. They see the hallmarks of it and can emulate it, much like a writer or painter emulates the greats.

AI assistants can give students lots of good examples. (Note that I didn't say "great" examples, but "good.") Ask them for an essay about a certain topic. Then ask again and again, and you'll get something different each time. When it's time for the student to create something of their own, much like an artist or musician studying the greats, they'll draw from the examples they've seen.

PROMPT TIP: You won't annoy the AI assistant if you ask it a lot. So don't hold back! Each time, ask for slight adjustments in the types of responses it gives.

⤧ 3. USE AI TO REMIX STUDENT WORK.

Students create something for class: a story, an essay, a poem, a recap of something they've learned. Then, they can ask an AI assistant to remix it for them.

Donnie Piercey, a Kentucky Teacher of the Year, did this with his fifth-grade students' work. He pasted a student's story into an AI assistant to remix it as a nursery rhyme, a soap opera, a sea shanty, and a children's book—with suggested illustrations!

What's the benefit for students? For one, it's fun! But it also opens their minds to new genres of reading and writing. When students see how their work has been remixed, they might want to emulate that type of writing in a future assignment. Those doors might not be opened if an AI assistant didn't help.

PROMPT TIP: Brainstorm lots of genres of writing with students to get more ways to remix their work.

 4. ADD AI TO THE "THINK-PAIR-SHARE" THINKING ROUTINE.

I love this line of thinking shared by education entrepreneur Sarah Dillard (Twitter: @dillardsarah), founder of Kaleidoscope Education. She wrote: "Augmenting the think-pair-share with ChatGPT could be one of the biggest tech-enabled leaps in pedagogy: Think. Pair. ChatGPT. Pair. Share."

Students think about a prompt, encouraging them to retrieve what they know from memory and consider it. Then they discuss it with a classmate. Then they do any searches they want with an AI assistant. They pair back up to discuss what they've found. Then they share with the class. The AI assistant adds an additional perspective and more information.

PROMPT TIP: Use this idea with other thinking routines, too. Find lots of them in Project Zero's Thinking Routines Toolbox at ditch.link/zero.

 5. GRADE THE AI.

Toronto-area educator Jen Giffen's high school students came up with this idea:

Give a writing prompt to an AI assistant. It could be a different writing prompt than you'll give your students. Then, read the essay the bot creates for you.

Next, give the students the rubric you use to grade their writing, and ask them to grade the response from the AI assistant.

This helps students to be reflective about the grading process—and about their own writing process. When students get grades on their own work, it's easy to take it personally—or to dismiss it because it makes them feel like they've messed up. But when they critique the work of a bot that doesn't have feelings, it eliminates a lot of those emotions.

PROMPT TIP: After the AI assistant writes the essay, copy and paste your rubric into the AI assistant. Ask it to grade its own work according to the rubric and provide feedback.

6. DEBATE THE AI.

This one also came from Jen Giffen's high school students: Let students (as individuals, in pairs or small groups, or even as a whole-group activity) debate an AI assistant.

Students take one side of a debate. The AI takes the other. Students plug their points in and ask the bot to rebut.

It gives them low-stakes practice—and as much practice as they want—to hone their debate skills. Plus, they may see talking points for their own stance (or that their opponent may use) so they can strengthen their argument.

PROMPT TIP: AI assistants can adjust their tones and language to match different ages and levels of understanding, so specify who you want it to respond as. It could be someone of your students' same age and grade level or someone with more expertise.

7. USE AI FOR INSIGHT INTO BIG, DIFFICULT-TO-SOLVE PROBLEMS.

If you and your students can't solve a big math or science problem (or don't want to take the time to solve it), ask an AI assistant for a solution.

If it can, the bot will show you an answer. But, more importantly, you'll gain some insight into the process of solving it. And even if it can't solve it, it'll tell you why. Analyzing how the AI assistant tackled the problem could be valuable in itself.

Also, you could also ask the AI assistant how to solve bigger societal problems just to see what it would say. I asked it how to solve world hunger, and here's what I got:

Eliminating world hunger is a complex and multifaceted challenge that requires the efforts of governments, international organizations, and individuals around the world. Some strategies that have been proposed to address this issue include:

Increasing agricultural productivity: This can be done through the use of advanced technologies such as precision farming and genetically modified crops, as well as by improving infrastructure and access to education and training for farmers.

Reducing food waste: Up to one-third of all food produced in the world is lost or wasted, which represents a significant opportunity to increase food availability. Reducing food waste can be achieved through better storage and transportation systems, as well as by increasing awareness about the issue.

Improving distribution systems: In many cases, food is available, but it is not distributed effectively to those who need it most. Improving distribution systems, including supply chains and transportation networks, can help get food to the people who need it.

Promoting economic development: Economic growth can lead to increased food production and greater access to food, as well as the resources and infrastructure needed to address food insecurity.

Providing emergency food aid: In times of crisis, such as during natural disasters or armed conflict, providing emergency food aid can help prevent starvation and malnutrition.

Ultimately, addressing world hunger will require a combination of these and other approaches, as well as strong political will and sustained commitment from governments and other organizations. Source: ChatGPT via chat.openai.com (2022)

PROMPT TIP: If you see holes in its logic or incomplete thoughts, ask it for a follow-up—or challenge its response!

 8. ASK AI FOR ADVICE.

Another suggestion from educator Jen Giffen: She asked ChatGPT very generally, "Give me some advice." It gave her some general (yet very good) ideas on managing stress, relationships, and mental well-being.

An AI assistant can't be a replacement for counseling or medical help. But we do take advice from friends, family...even strangers sometimes. If students (or teachers) are struggling with just about anything, they can get advice from this artificial intelligence—an AI that's working with much of the entirety of the internet as its dataset.

PROMPT TIP: Specify your goals—what you want to accomplish with the advice—to narrow the results and make them more helpful.

 9. ANTICIPATE THE RESPONSE YOU'D EXPECT FROM AI.

If your students have been studying a topic, ask them how they think an AI assistant would summarize that topic—what facts would it include, what wouldn't it include, and in what order would it provide them. This exercise could be a great retrieval/brain dump activity, helping students recall what they remember to build long-term memory. It can also encourage them to think critically by justifying the order of importance in how they think AI will respond.

A practical way to do this in the classroom is to use our Be the Bot templates for Google Slides and PowerPoint. On the template, provide the students with the prompt(s) you'll ask the AI assistant later. The students write out what they think the AI assistant will say. Then, when you query the AI assistant later, students can compare their versions and analyze them. Make a copy of the free Be the Bot template to use in class at ditch.link/bethebot.

PROMPT TIP: If your students come up with a very different response than the AI assistant produces, ask the assistant why it didn't say what your students say for feedback.

 10. TAKE SEVERAL AI RESPONSES AND MAKE A BETTER PRODUCT.

AI assistants often have a button that says "regenerate response." Each time you ask it a question, it generates an original response from the same prompt, doing the work from scratch every time. (If you can't find a button like that, just ask the question again—or ask the AI assistant for another response.)

If you were asked to pick a movie as your favorite, describe it, and explain why you like it in 60 seconds, your response would be a little different each time. (For me, the movie would probably be different every time!) It's an original, unique work each time. AI assistants work kind of like that every time.

Ask it to answer a question or write something for you. Then ask it again...and again...and again. Get five (or more!) versions of the same prompt.

Have students (individually, in pairs/small groups, or even ask a class) take the best parts from those versions and turn them into a better final product.

Here's a practical application of this: our Frankenbot template for Google Slides and PowerPoint. It's called "Frankenbot" from Frankenstein (assembled from pieces of many sources) and bot (from an artificial intelligence source). Use an AI assistant to generate multiple responses to a writing prompt. Paste them on the template, which you provide to students. Then, students pick the best parts from the AI responses to assemble their final product. Afterward, they reflect on the writing decisions they made.

This can be a scaffolding strategy for students who struggle to write essays or papers. It introduces them to some of the strategies for crafting a written work without all of the taxing effort of doing the whole thing. Make a copy of the free Frankenbot template to use in class at ditch.link/frankenbot.

PROMPT TIP: Ask the assistant for variation among the responses it generates—for different age levels, more or less complex, in a different tone, etc.

11. USE AI TO CREATE PERSONALIZED LEARNING EXPERIENCES.

The source of this idea is ChatGPT. I asked, "How can AI be used to help teach in the classroom?" It gave me lots of suggestions. This example is more focused on general AI, and I think it's definitely coming:

"AI can be used to create personalized learning experiences for students by adapting the content and pace of instruction to each student's needs and abilities. This can be achieved through the use of adaptive learning software, which adjusts the material based on the student's performance." Source: ChatGPT via chat.openai.com (2022)

The more AI tools spread into existing classroom tech tools, the more this will become possible. Even right now, as of the publication of this book, when there aren't as many options for this readily available, some AI tools and assistants can help us do this just by asking them for recommendations and ideas.

PROMPT TIP: Some back and forth from the AI assistant can get the results you need. Describe the student's situation, and if the results aren't a good fit, tell it how to adjust.

12. USE AI TO FACILITATE GROUP WORK.

This response came from ChatGPT. It's not very elegant as-is, but it's a novel way to use AI to help with the administration of learning tasks in the classroom.

"I can facilitate group work by assigning tasks to each group and keeping track of their progress. I can also provide feedback on the quality of their work and suggest ways to improve." Source: ChatGPT via chat.openai.com (2023)

It said it could create groups of students, assign them tasks, monitor progress, provide feedback, and encourage collaboration. It said that the teacher would need to input all of the data to get its recommendations and provide the information to the students. If you're teaching a subject that's new to you—or something you've been assigned that you don't know much about—AI assistants could help you drive group work forward and make suggestions you might not think of.

PROMPT TIP: If you're teaching content you're not familiar with, picture the AI assistant as an experienced teacher. Ask the assistant the types of questions you'd ask that experienced teacher.

 13. PROVIDE A UNIQUE PERSPECTIVE WITH AI.

Want to know how someone from history—or someone with a unique perspective—might think or respond to a question? Educator Jonny Franks shared on Twitter (Twitter: @mrfranks): "I've used it for generating counter arguments in Philosophy lessons and as a Buddhist monk interviewee in a Religious Studies lesson."

This kind of activity could help students see a concept from a different perspective. However, like so many AI-enriched activities, take caution. The view an AI assistant might think that someone would take is based on the information in its dataset and not on the lived experience of a human being. Pair an activity like this with some critical thinking and conversation about how accurate the students think the response is.

PROMPT TIP: Describe the perspective it should emulate. If its responses aren't hitting the mark, tell it how to adjust.

14. USE AI TO APPLY LEARNING IN UNFORGETTABLE WAYS.

The boundless creativity of AI assistants opens up lots of doors and helps us capture students' attention and engage them in ways they won't forget.

Educator Dana shared on Twitter (Twitter: @Da-natellaBella): "We used it to write a rap about similes and metaphors. Then, we edited the rap and put our own beat to it."

Raps. Poems. Haikus. Songs. Dialogue. Even jokes. You'll never know what creative responses these AI assistants can make if you don't ask them. Then, like

Dana did, the students and teacher can personalize and remix the results to suit their needs—and even put it to a beat!

PROMPT TIP: Tell it to include certain vocabulary words or concepts that are important to the lesson.

15. EMPOWER STUDENTS TO MAKE A DIFFERENCE IN THE WORLD.

More and more students are attempting to solve real-world problems and find real-world applications of their learning. Unfortunately, that doesn't guarantee that those solutions and applications will work effectively. A little guidance from an AI assistant might help refine their work. Here's how educator Krista Fancher (Twitter: @KristaFancher) described it on Twitter:

"A student loaded a social entrepreneurship project from last year and asked ChatGPT to find everything wrong with the solution. It did. He used the list of flaws to redesign the project and built a new prototype designed to connect grandparents and their grandchildren. Amazing!"

PROMPT TIP: If an AI assistant suggests changes, you can ask it to create a new version that implements the changes it suggests.

16. HELP PERSUASIVE WRITING WITH AI.

Persuading others takes some skill. Sometimes, it's helpful for students to get a starting point and adjust it as necessary. Here's how educator Kelly Duncan (Twitter: @hijolepues on Twitter) described his students' use of AI to do that: "(Students have) been using it today to write scripts for PSAs and short films in our Principles of A/V Tech course."

PROMPT TIP: Ask the AI assistant for suggested images or videos—as well as types of background music—to accompany these videos. Then ask it to tell you why it made those selections.

17. USE AI TO IMPROVE VOCABULARY.

One use of AI we'll likely see for years is to improve what we've created. An obvious benefit is that it can make the text we write better. But it can help us become better writers, too. When AI attempts to improve student writing, students can reflect on the changes that an AI assistant made to their work—and reverse engineer them as strategies to use for the next time they write.

The IB English Guys shared this idea in a collaborative document full of ideas: "Students write an essay.

Copy/paste the essay into an AI assistant, asking it to improve the vocabulary. Observe the changes and reflect on them. Are they better or worse?"

PROMPT TIP: Ask the AI assistant to elevate the student's writing to a more complex level (i.e., college level) or even a more simple level (i.e., of a fourth grader).

FOR PLANNING, GRADING, AND TEACHER TASKS

18. ASK AI FOR DEFINITIONS ON A VARIETY OF LEVELS.

If you need a concept explained or defined, an AI assistant can provide that explanation—and do it in as detailed or simple a manner as you'd like.

On episode 99 of the *Partial Credit Podcast*, Jesse Lubinsky shared that he asked for a definition of "faith" in terms a child would understand. That helped me realize that it can give definitions, descriptions, and explanations (which we expected) and level them up or down in complexity.

Educator Alona Fyshe (Twitter: @alonamarie) explained it this way on Twitter: "I used it to get a better definition of intentionality. I asked it to explain it to me like I was 5 and it was slightly better than how I had been trying to explain it."

PROMPT TIP: You can give an AI assistant a definition from a textbook or a definition you commonly use yourself. Then, ask it to improve it, to make it easier to understand, or to provide an analogy.

19. ASK AI FOR TEXT IN A VARIETY OF VOICES.

This is a mash-up of the earlier definitions and perspectives ideas. AI tools can help create lots of additional reading content in the voice of all sorts of people. Examples: characters from a book, people in history, types of people you'd meet today, and people from a certain location. Ask it to write a poem in the style of Emily Dickinson or E. E. Cummings.

Another twist: Ask it to respond in the style of certain writers, poets, rappers, etc. This also opens the door to having back-and-forth conversations with those people. For example, I asked ChatGPT to respond to the statement "dogs are better than cats" in a way US president Barack Obama would.

Here's my paraphrase of the four-paragraph response it gave in Obama's style:

While I respect your opinion, I believe that dogs and cats both have unique qualities that make them special. Dogs are known for loyalty and enthusiasm, and many have impacted their families and communities. At the same time, cats are affectionate and playful and have a quiet elegance and grace. While I understand that some may have a preference, I believe that both dogs and cats have a place in our lives and hearts.

When I asked how that response was in Obama's style, ChatGPT noted that it's measured and respectful and seeks to find common ground, as Obama does. It's not dismissive, and it's well-articulated and thoughtful, focusing on bringing people together.

Responses like this can create great classroom discussion and debate.

PROMPT TIP: To see someone's writing style in practice, ask students to write a simple essay on a basic topic. Then, ask an AI assistant to reword it in a particular person's style (like I did above with Barack Obama).

 20. ASK AI FOR STUDENT WORK FEEDBACK.

We know that one key aspect of effective feedback is that it's timely. With traditional paper-based work, students turn it in and must wait for teachers to grade it—and return it!—before they can see feedback. Lots of edtech tools are letting us get feedback to students more quickly—whether automated or through direct communication with a teacher or classmate.

AI assistants can be another source of feedback. When students finish written work, they can copy/paste it into an AI assistant and ask how they can improve their writing. For example, I copied one of my blog posts into ChatGPT and simply asked how I could improve it. It gave me a list of five suggestions, including transitional phrases, adding more examples, and breaking it up into shorter paragraphs. (Better start a new paragraph now...)

A human touch is important here, though. It's up to the student—based on what they have learned about writing—to decide whether to implement the advice and how. Plus, a teacher would want to weigh in on whether the suggestions given by the AI assistant are appropriate in the context of the class and the student's writing.

PROMPT TIP: If you have a rubric, copy and submit it to the AI assistant before providing student work, asking it to provide feedback based on that rubric.

21. ASK AI TO DO SOME TEACHER TASKS FOR YOU.

AI assistants can write lesson plans for you. Or some questions for a quiz. Ask it for some jokes about your content so you can slip those into class. Of course, you don't have to use everything it provides you verbatim. But it might give you a starting point that you can modify, or if you already have something, it can give you ideas to improve.

PROMPT TIP: Tell the AI assistant what you like and dislike about its response to get more of the good and less of the bad.

 ## 22. CREATE REVIEW CONTENT, QUESTIONS, AND ACTIVITIES WITH AI.

Writing quiz questions, content for flashcards, and other review work can be a chore. It's already pretty formulaic, and lots of it doesn't take a ton of deep thought. If we can outsource some of it to artificial intelligence, it can save us time. Copy and paste notes from a lesson or content that students have studied into an AI assistant and ask it to:

- Summarize the text.
- Write quiz questions (open-ended, multiple choice, etc.).

- Create discussion prompts.
- Create short definitions or descriptions for flash cards.
- Offer memory aids or mnemonic devices.
- Suggest new ways to organize or group material.

PROMPT TIP: Give the AI assistant specifics on how you'd like it to format the content to make it easier to move to another app or website.

 23. WRITE REPORT CARD COMMENTS AND PARENT EMAILS WITH AI HELP.

To be clear, we don't want to haphazardly ask an AI assistant to tell parents how their student is performing in class. But it can give us a starting point. We can provide the AI chatbot with some details of the situation and ask for an email, comment, or message that could be sent to a parent. We can also ask it to write in a specific tone. Once we have that starting point, we can adjust as necessary, adding new details and fixing what doesn't sound right. Then, when we have a result that works, we can send it.

PROMPT TIP: Copy and paste a previous email or previous comments to provide the AI assistant with context before it creates comments or emails for you this time.

24. USE AI TO SUMMARIZE TEXTS.

If a text your students are reading is in the dataset of ChatGPT (or a similar tool), they could always try to ask it for a summary of the whole thing—or of certain chapters, sections, acts, scenes, etc. This is what we used SparkNotes and CliffsNotes for years ago. Of course, SparkNotes and CliffsNotes were controversial in the past—"if they read those, they'll never read the text!"—but eventually, we found ways they could support learning, too.

Seeing a summary of a text that you've just read can help you process what you've read. It's similar in nature to a book club. You hear what other people think and observe about the text, and it helps inform your view of it.

PROMPT TIP: To have a better chance at getting what you're looking for, tell the AI assistant what to focus on when creating the summary.

 25. USE AI TO CREATE LEVELED TEXT SETS.

What if you could generate different versions of the same text but on different reading levels? Educator Brittany Ferguson (Twitter: @BFergusonVB) did this to help differentiate reading materials for her students. Here's how she explained it on Twitter: "I used it today to create leveled text sets: fiction, nonfiction, and poetry with our science and social studies unit using the essential knowledge. Literally saved hours and hours of resource curation."

PROMPT TIP: If the response you get is too simple or complex, ask it for another version that's a little more simple or complex. You can also ask it to include key vocabulary words, literary devices, etc.

 ## 26. GENERATE PROMPTS AND QUESTIONS WITH AI TO FACILITATE DISCUSSIONS.

We want students to think, discuss, and respond, but an AI assistant can help us frame and facilitate those discussions. Educator Tom Spall (Twitter: @Tommyspall) suggested using it "to formulate possible discussion points, questions, topics, and misconceptions for collaborative discussions."

I asked ChatGPT, "How can you (ChatGPT) be used to help teach in the classroom?"

The response: "I can be used to facilitate discussions among students by posing questions and prompts that encourage critical thinking and encourage stu-

dents to engage with the material in a deeper way."
Source: ChatGPT via chat.openai.com (2022)

PROMPT TIP: To get a preview of how the discussion might go (or a direction you'd like to steer the discussion), ask it for responses to your discussion points, questions, etc.

 27. USE AI AS A VIRTUAL LAB.

AI assistants can serve as a virtual lab, doing calculations based on a variety of specifications. For example, I asked ChatGPT to serve as a virtual lab about projectile motion. It simulated a cannon firing a ball after I gave it the initial velocity of the ball, the angle in degrees, the mass of the ball, and the air resistance. It gave me estimates of the maximum height of the ball, the time taken to reach maximum height, as well as the horizontal distance traveled and time taken before the ball hit the ground.

I asked it to serve as a virtual lab, described what I wanted it to simulate, and told it to ask me for the specifications necessary to conduct the experiment.

If it can do that kind of simulation, imagine what else you could ask it to simulate.

PROMPT TIP: If you're not sure the AI assistant can run the virtual lab you imagine, ask it if it can and what information it would need to make it happen.

28. CREATE PRESENTATION SLIDES WITH AI.

If Google Slides or PowerPoint slides are part of your teaching life, AI assistants can help. Ask the AI assistant to generate text you'd include on all of the slides—and tell it how many slides you want to create. You can copy and paste from teaching notes or any resources you have. Or you could ask it to create text for slides on a certain topic to see what it comes up with.

PROMPT TIP: Ask it to suggest images to use on the slide, too. Or go beyond a general AI assistant and experiment with some of the AI slide-creation tools that are available.

29. WRITE CONTENT FOR INDIVIDUALIZED EDUCATIONAL PLANS (IEPS) WITH AI.

Paperwork has always been the bane of the existence of special education teachers. Creating all the documentation for individualized educational plans

(IEPs) can keep teachers from doing the actual work necessary to support their students. Oklahoma educator Tiffany Peltier (Twitter: @tiffany_peltier) posted an IEP goal she generated through ChatGPT on Twitter. She requested a goal for a child in the fourth grade who was reading at 21 words per minute. It created the goal and then provided a rationale for that goal. The discussion that ensued included special ed teachers sharing more ideas and implementations. You can find it at ditch.link/aiforieps.

PROMPT TIP: Don't stop with IEPs! Ask AI assistants to help you with any tedious paperwork you need. Have it create a starting point and then edit and adjust as necessary.

30. USE AI TO HELP WRITE LETTERS OF RECOMMENDATION.

As a high school teacher, I know the struggle of keeping up with requests from students to write letters of recommendation. After you write enough of them, they all start to sound the same. AI assistants can be a great place to create a baseline letter that you can customize and improve to meet your needs. Provide context for the letter, like what it's for, who the audience is, and what's important, and ask it to write it for you. Include highlights about the student you want to include, what attributes to emphasize, and the tone you want to strike.

PROMPT TIP: If the student sends you a digital resume or CV, copy and paste it into the AI assistant. Then, ask it to write a letter of recommendation.

MORE AI TOOLS AND IDEAS

In this section, we've covered 30 ways to use AI assistants to support teaching and learning. As AI use becomes more widespread and mainstream, it will impact teaching and learning in many more ways. Other types of AI tools include slide deck creators, lesson plan generators, quiz generators, speech evaluators, grammar checkers, image generators, and more. Check out other ways that AI can impact your classroom at ditch.link/aitools.

KEY DEFINITION

DATASET

A collection of data used to train artificial intelligence. It's all of the information gathered to teach an AI and help it learn how to respond.

Here's an example dataset:

Imagine a spreadsheet that logs the results of coin flips. It keeps track of how many times the coin is flipped and what the result is—heads or tails. Imagine that process being replicated millions of times in a virtual environment. AI can use those results—and what it's learned from other datasets it has access to—to tell you that choosing neither heads nor tails yields any sort of competitive advantage. Of course, AI is only as good as its dataset and the training it has done. Like humans, AI and its datasets have limitations, biases, and even inaccuracies. More training and more data can improve those deficiencies.

 Bot Check: 80% human created, 20% artificial intelligence created.

 Used AI to: Generate a few classroom ideas, write a definition of "dataset" that I edited, test out lots of the human-created examples.

Find shareable infographics like the one on the next page at:
AIforEDUbook.com

30 WAYS AI CAN SUPPORT TEACHING AND LEARNING

AI FOR EDUCATORS

MATT MILLER

Use AI as a deeper source of information than Google.

Use AI for lots of good examples.

Use AI to remix student work.

Add AI to the "think pair share" thinking routine.

Grade the AI.

Debate the AI.

Use AI for insight into big, difficult-to-solve problems.

Ask AI for advice.

Anticipate the response you'd expect from AI.

Take several AI responses and make a better product.

Use AI to create personalized learning experiences.

Use AI to facilitate group work.

Provide a unique perspective with AI.

Use AI to apply learning in unforgettable ways.

Empower students to make a difference in the world.

Help persuasive writing with AI.

Use AI to improve vocabulary.

Ask AI for definitions on a variety of levels.

Ask AI for text in a variety of voices.

Ask AI for student work feedback.

Ask AI to do some teacher tasks for you.

Create review content, questions, and activities with AI.

Write report card comments and parent emails with AI help.

Use AI to summarize texts.

Use AI to create leveled text sets.

Generate prompts and questions with AI to facilitate discussions.

Use AI as a virtual lab.

Create presentation slides with AI.

Write content for individualized educational plans (IEPs) with AI.

Use AI to help write letters of recommendation.

Infographic provided by Ditch That Textbook. Learn more at AIforEduBook.com

DITCH THAT TEXTBOOK

WHAT ARE CHEATING AND PLAGIARISM ANYMORE?

ENCOURAGING ACADEMIC HONESTY IN THE FACE OF AI CONTENT CREATION

Some say: Block it. Ban it. Stop the cheating. Stop plagiarism. Others say: Embrace it. Adapt. Prepare students. Evolve.

Talk to educators about the proliferation of artificial intelligence, and you're likely to find them on either of these two polar opposite sides of the discussion—or somewhere thoughtfully in between.

Most of us realize that it's going to cause things to change and impact education. In a reader survey about AI in education, one reader's succinct opinion stood out to me:

"It is unavoidable whether I'm excited or not."

So, how do we navigate these muddy waters of a world of AI? How do we help prepare students to thrive and succeed—yet maintain responsibility and grow as human beings?

Let's go back to that reader survey I did for a second. With more than 300 responses to it, I learned a lot. I conducted it in February 2023. (Remember, in some ways, this book is a snapshot in time.) At that time, 74.6% of respondents said their interest in learning about AI and its implications in education was 5 out of 5 (most interested). Also, 73.7% chose to hear about AI "very often/a lot" or "fairly often."

In that survey, educators from all over the world shared their feelings and findings, questions and qualms about the future of education with AI in it.

In this chapter, I'll paraphrase and combine many of those readers' responses into a conversation. Let's see if you see yourself in it.

I have such mixed emotions about all of this AI stuff. I want to be at the forefront, and I know that this is a big part of my students' future. But there's a lot to be concerned about.

I'm the same. I get excited about the future and the possibilities of artificial intelligence, but it also scares me. It's a disruption, for sure. Over time, the presence of AI is going to change what our assignments look like, what we ask of students, and what we're preparing them for. It doesn't have to change completely right now. There's no need to panic. Plus, it's going to take us some time to figure out what our new normal looks like. We can only do the best we can with what we know now. It's like that famous Maya Angelou quote: "Do the best you can until you know better. Then when you know better, do better."

My biggest concern right now is cheating. I still want my students to learn and think. I'm worried that they'll just plug my assignments into an AI assistant mindlessly and won't learn anything.

In my opinion, it's really good that we're talking about the importance of thinking. With AI assistants in our world, we still need human brains, human eyes, and human hearts to make sure that what they're generating is appropriate, helpful, and practical.

I believe that "thinking" and "using AI" are not mutually exclusive. They can both be done at the same time. Hopefully, that's clear after the ideas for using it we explored in previous chapters.

For now, let's address that word: "cheating." Many sources describe cheating as acting dishonestly or unfairly to gain an advantage over others—or, in this case, over the standard of learning we want them to achieve.

I think society's definition of the word "cheating" is going to morph as AI assimilates into our work and personal lives. It's a tool that will help us be more productive. It will be used in the work world. (It already is.) To prepare students for the future, they need to learn how to integrate AI into their work ethically and responsibly while using their humanity as an advantage. We don't want students to graduate high school or college and realize that any skills they have are already obsolete.

In schools, we're going to have to think hard about what we consider cheating. And we'll have to define it in terms of our students' futures—and not our present, nor our current status quo practices in the classroom.

How do we define cheating with AI? It's tricky, and it's something teachers, schools, and school districts will need to talk and think about.

Rethinking "plagiarism" and "cheating"

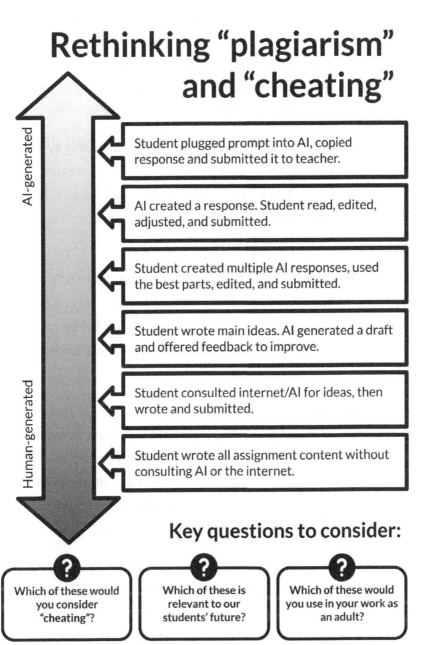

AI-generated

Student plugged prompt into AI, copied response and submitted it to teacher.

AI created a response. Student read, edited, adjusted, and submitted.

Student created multiple AI responses, used the best parts, edited, and submitted.

Student wrote main ideas. AI generated a draft and offered feedback to improve.

Student consulted internet/AI for ideas, then wrote and submitted.

Student wrote all assignment content without consulting AI or the internet.

Human-generated

Key questions to consider:

? Which of these would you consider "cheating"?

? Which of these is relevant to our students' future?

? Which of these would you use in your work as an adult?

Graphic by Matt Miller (@jmattmiller) DitchThatTextbook.com

DITCH THAT TEXTBOOK

Let's consider it this way. Take a look at this graphic, where the work being done ranges from completely AI-created to completely human-created. Somewhere, we'll have to draw the line and say, "This is cheating." That is, we're saying, "This is not aligned with the standards we hold for our students."

► At the top of the graphic is **work that's done only by AI** without any thinking by the student. Is that cheating? I think it's safe to say that this isn't what we want for our students. They're not doing any thinking, so it isn't developing skills that will serve them in the future.

► At the bottom of the graphic is **work that's done only by humans** without the aid of the internet or AI. We may not consider that cheating, but it's problematic. Why? Because this kind of work isn't authentic to our students' futures. I don't think that's exactly what we want.

► Everything in the middle of those two is **the AI/human gray area.** In this area, somewhere, is authentic work that prepares students for tomorrow while also stimulating their thinking and learning. But it's up to interpretation. Where do you draw the line? What kind of work promotes the kind of learning that will serve students?

► Amid these conversations, we also have to ask ourselves this: **Which of these would you use in your work as an adult?** Why would we hold students to a different standard, especially if our work as an adult is a partial reflection of the kind of work they'll do one day?

► Here's more food for thought. Education leader Ken Shelton saw this graphic and added this provocation: "**Replace the term 'AI' in this graphic with 'classmate' or 'friend' at school,** and does your opinion/perspective change?" We need to have these conversations about collaborative work, too.

I see what you're saying about changes to the term "cheating" and preparing students for the future. I've been thinking a lot about that. But I still want my students to write. And to think. I already have to grade essays and check for plagiarism. Now, I need to worry about AI, too. I just don't have time for all of that.

There are a couple of things at play here. Let's talk about "plagiarism" and detecting it for a moment. Right now, a common definition of "plagiarism" is: taking someone else's work or ideas and passing them off as your own.

When an AI assistant writes something, it does the work originally every time. Plagiarism is based on using a human's work as your own. Intellectual property is "any product of the human intellect that the law protects from unauthorized use by others" (Cornell Law School, n.d.).

Though this may change as the law adapts to suit technological advances and challenges, currently, work created by artificial intelligence isn't intellectual property owned by anyone. In some ways, it's like work that's released in the public domain, which is not bound by copyright and can be reused by anyone, without attribution, for any purpose. Ask an AI assistant who owns the response it just gave you. It'll likely tell you that it's not human and it can't own that intellectual property. Ask it how you should cite its work, and it'll probably tell you to identify the sources of the information and when you retrieved it (as we do when we cite internet resources).

Again, definitions are important, right? We talked about the changing definition of "cheating." The definition of "plagiarism"—and academic policies about it—may morph as well. Hopefully, though, as they change, they reflect the skills and realities students will face in the real world and not past or present realities we want to hold on to for nostalgia or stubbornness.

I can't eliminate the time burden of checking for academic honesty. We can start to see AI as a tool that students will use (much like search engines) and encourage responsible use of it. When we do that, we'll spend less time fighting against it and more time helping students prepare for their future.

That's good in theory, but I need more practical answers than that. My students will say, "This is my essay. I wrote it." How do I prove it if it's not?

OK, let's talk about AI detectors—the first answer that comes to lots of people's minds.

In the days and weeks after ChatGPT and AI assistants were released, there was instant demand for AI detectors. And, as it does, the market supplied for the demand. A quick internet search for "AI detectors" or "GPT detectors" yields plenty of results.

But wait. Before you rush to the internet and search, you have to ask: Do they really solve the problem? (And, bigger picture, what do we see as a problem? And is the perceived problem really a problem?)

Let's put it this way. When TurnItIn came on the scene, it didn't "solve plagiarism." It didn't make plagiarism go away. It didn't force students to engage with the work or change their motivation, either.

OpenAI CEO Sam Altman addressed AI detectors in a 2023 interview (Loizos), saying:

"There may be ways we can help teachers be a little more likely to detect (AI-written work), but honestly, a determined person is going to get around them, and *I don't think it'll be something society can or should rely on long-term."*

Here are some things to consider regarding AI detectors:

▶ **AI detectors are not a cure-all.** Even if you found the most accurate, effective one, it wouldn't keep students from using AI to do their work, and it won't make AI tools disappear.

▶ **Today's AI detectors aren't very reliable.** They routinely produce false positives, saying human-created text was created by AI, and false negatives, the inverse. Just like in court, you can't accuse someone using evidence that isn't reliable.

▶ **They can be the beginning of a discussion.** If a student turns in work that appears to be heavily AI-generated, it might be time to talk. How do I know what you've learned? Are there barriers preventing you from doing the work yourself? In a world with more and more AI, how will you leverage your humanity, so you're not outsourced by AI?

▶ **Use your teacher eyes and teacher brain.** If you've been reading your students' work and following their progress, your human senses might detect that something doesn't look or sound like them better than an AI checker could.

We're making a little progress. I see that the definitions of cheating and plagiarism are changing, and I know that AI detectors won't fix everything. But I'm still worried that AI is going to write my students' essays for them.

Let's just be honest. They might. That's why we need to have conversations with students about how to ethically and responsibly use AI for learning. (And let's be honest again. Even if we have those conversations, some will still use it irresponsibly.)

So, how do we modify our teaching? How do we bring essays into a world with AI integrated? Honestly, the answer to this question doesn't just apply to essays. It's a line of thought that will work for many kinds of student work.

To move forward, we have to ask a foundational question: why do we ask students to write essays in the first place? What is their purpose in education?

Essays are tools we've used to understand what students understand. What they can do. How they see the world. What their process is. In the past (and the present), they have helped us peer inside our students' brains to see what they've learned and how they think.

Essays have also been great ways for students to practice communication. They give students practice at writing, which hones the skill of developing an idea and communicating it in a clear and effective way that others can understand.

This isn't to say that essays are totally obsolete because of AI assistants. When students do the cognitive work themselves (or with an appropriate amount of technology support), they're still a great intellectual exercise.

We have to come to terms with two things:

► Traditional essays may be influenced by AI to varying degrees from now on.

► If we assign essays, we have to accept the risk that students may try to avoid thinking by over-relying on AI assistants.

Other ways of measuring student learning and practicing communication exist beyond essays. (Chapters 4 and 5 in this book have some suggestions.)

You still haven't come up with a way for me to keep students from having AI do their work for them.

You're right. I haven't. And I can't. And you can't. Ever since the dawn of education, students who are not motivated—who are not engaged in the work—have found ways of avoiding work they don't want to do. There's a good chance that during discussions with Socrates himself, some of his students' minds drifted and they stared into space. The truth is that if students aren't motivated, they'll eventually find a reason to disengage. That's not an indictment on the teacher or the teaching. It's just a fact. In this case, AI might be the way they disengage. It becomes our job to find out why they're disengaging and to make changes—to our teaching, to the student's source of motivation, etc.

Well, my school district has blocked ChatGPT. Plus, you have to be 18 or older to use ChatGPT (or 13 or older with parental permission), so my students can't use it anyway.

It's true that (as of the publication of this book) users have to be 18 or older to use ChatGPT or 13 or older with a parent or guardian's consent. I'd say your school district is doing its job by blocking any app or site that requires its users to be older than most will be while enrolled in your district. It would be great if your district allowed it for teachers, though.

Let's also be clear about something else. Even if the terms of use have age restrictions, students younger than that will still use it outside the classroom. (They might even access it on their phones inside the classroom—or in the hallway, or in the restroom...) It's like social media. Age restrictions and terms of service rarely scare kids away from using them. We can't require students to use tools they're not old enough to use, but blocking them at school also won't create a bubble where they'll never touch it until they're 18.

Also, those 18+ terms of use are for just one product—ChatGPT. Lots of other AI assistants and other AI tools will come around, and eventually, some may have younger terms of use. Some of these products will eventually be embedded in the tech tools and apps that students use. Students will have access to them legally at some point. We have to be careful not to let the age restrictions of one product dismiss us from having conversations about the role of AI.

If we don't have discussions about and model appropriate and responsible use of AI, students won't have those skills and understanding when they graduate high school, go to college, and move on to the work world. We're putting them at a disadvantage if we don't equip them to effectively use AI.

OK. This conversation helps. I still have concerns, though. I mean, this conjures visions of SkyNet—you know, that artificial superintelligence system from *The Terminator* movies that became self-aware and tried to destroy the world? We need to tread lightly.

You should have concerns. So do I. And we do need to tread lightly. There's a lot to consider, and it's not all sunshine and rainbows. I'm an optimist by nature and focus too much on the positives. It's easy to do. We should hold those concerns close but also allow room for the possibilities and doors all of this opens.

In the next chapter, we're going to discuss some of the ethical considerations we face in a world of integrated AI—and some conversations you can have with your students.

KEY DEFINITION

MACHINE LEARNING

When machines or computers create step-by-step instructions (algorithms) based on learning from datasets and lots of practice. The system learns from data, identifies patterns, and then makes predictions and decisions based on all of that learning. The more data it gets and the more practice it gets with that data, the better it gets at creating the desired outcome.

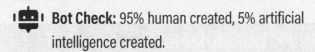

Bot Check: 95% human created, 5% artificial intelligence created.

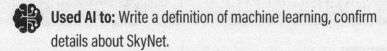

Used AI to: Write a definition of machine learning, confirm details about SkyNet.

Find bonus resources, shareable infographics, and more at:
AIforEDUbook.com

ACTING RESPONSIBLY IN AN AI-INTEGRATED WORLD

MAINTAINING OUR HUMANITY AND ETHICS AS AI EXPANDS

Thinking about artificial intelligence can make our skin crawl.

This is the visceral reaction I've had when discussing AI and its implementation with friends, family, and colleagues. Some of it is based on a lack of knowledge—the fear of the unknown. But a lot of it is based on ethics.

We try to picture a world where AI spreads into different spheres of life and we ask, "Does this look good? How could it hurt or harm what we hold sacred?"

Here's a good start: learning about and discussing those things that make our skin crawl.

The 193 member states of UNESCO (United Nations Educational, Scientific and Cultural Organization) adopted the Recommendation on the Ethics of Artificial Intelligence (2022), creating what it calls "the very first global standard-setting instrument on the subject."

It's a 141-point, 44-page document that identifies values, principles, areas of policy action, and more, created to "guide AI technologies in a responsible direction." It's a great starting point for educating oneself and creating discussion questions for classrooms, teaching staff, communities, and society.

Check it out. Ask questions. Dig for answers.

Here are some of the questions that are top of mind for me:

WHAT'S THE SOURCE OF THE DATA?

Any artificial intelligence system is only as good as its dataset—and the training it gets to use that dataset effectively.

There's an old maxim in computer programming: "garbage in, garbage out." If the programming is faulty, the results it produces will be just as faulty.

The dataset for any artificial intelligence is pulled from a variety of sources, but there's no way to encapsulate the entirety of information, perspectives, and experiences of all of humanity. There are going to be gaps. Plus, the sources of data are going to be fraught with bias and inaccuracy. (More on that in a moment.)

> **"Every system is perfectly designed to get the results it gets."**
> **—W. Edwards Deming**

The quote, "Every system is perfectly designed to get the results it gets," is often attributed to the engineer W. Edwards Deming. It doesn't always produce the results the designer wants. It produces the results it's designed to produce. If a system—like artificial intelligence—produces flawed results, it's exposing flaws in its data, the way it's trained, the way it was designed, etc.

The more you probe an artificial intelligence tool with queries, the more flaws you'll expose. This doesn't necessarily mean we shouldn't use artificial intelligence because it has gaps, biases, and inaccuracies. It just means we need to be aware of them so we can interpret the results and use what it produces in an appropriate way.

WHAT DATA IS IT COLLECTING?

This question takes me back to a TV series my wife and I have watched and re-watched called *Person of Interest*. In it, a software developer creates an artificial superintelligence called "The Machine." It's fed all sorts of personal data from unsuspecting people—public records, surveillance camera feeds, phone calls, emails, and more. "The Machine" was intended to detect threats to national security—threats the government deems "relevant." The software developer, Harold Finch, starts using it to find threats to ordinary people instead—people deemed "irrelevant"—to save their lives.

The show is chock full of ethical questions about surveillance, artificial intelligence, and the motives behind those controlling them (and what happens if the humans lose control).

In the show, clearly, "The Machine" processed data that was obtained illegally. But it brings to mind lots of questions we should be asking about AI today:

- ► What data is being collected by AI—and how is it being used?
- ► What personal data is being collected, and does it align with privacy laws (particularly child privacy laws)?
- ► What other data is being collected? By what means? Is it being collected ethically?

WHO IS WRITING THE ALGORITHM?

This question conjures images of the movie *The Wizard of Oz*. Dorothy finds herself in the land of Oz and wants to return home to Kansas. The wizard claimed to be able to help her if she met his demands. He appears to be a big, green, mysterious figure in a grand palace in Emerald City.

At one point in the movie, though, it's revealed that he's just an ordinary man, projecting the imposing image in the palace to create power and manipulate people. When Dorothy reveals him, he says an iconic line in the wizard's overpowering voice: "Pay no attention to that man behind the curtain!"

Behind all of the power was one man, making the decisions and pulling the strings.

We have to ask: who is writing the algorithm that drives artificial intelligence? Who is pulling the strings and making the decisions? Someone decides what's included in an algorithm, what's important, what's not, and what kind of result the AI creates. All of those decisions have consequences. And those decisions are being made by humans—humans with biases, with limited life experiences, with specific perspectives. Representation matters. Even if every type of person isn't represented as an employee working on AI products, their feedback should be.

Ken Shelton, a leader in equity conversations in education, asks: Who gets to define the term "intelligence?" What's the definition of intelligence, and who does it benefit? This is why it's key to have transparency in the creation of AI and representation of gender, race, background, and perspective to make sure no one's voice is silenced.

HOW ACCURATE IS IT?

When a new artificial intelligence tool is introduced to the world, it's not intended to be a perfect finished product. It needs to be trained. It gets better with more repetitions and interactions with humans.

It's not like an art exhibit. The artist toils over her painting in private, working and crafting and perfecting it until it's exactly as she wants. Then, she reveals the end result for all to see.

Instead, most artificial intelligence tools are more like a puppy. When a puppy is born, although cute, it is anything but a finished product. It promptly chews your furniture, pees on your floor, and barks all night to keep you up. Puppies are full of flaws, but the more you train them, the better they behave. And if you train them well, they learn to do tricks and follow your commands, so they're helpful. Well-trained puppies grow into responsible dogs.

We have two things to remember about accuracy. The first: no AI tool is supposed to be perfect from the start. ChatGPT was unveiled in a "free research preview," not as a finished product. When Google and Microsoft unveiled their first AI chatbots to rival OpenAI's ChatGPT, they were full of mistakes. In fact, Google's AI chatbot, Bard, made a high-profile mistake in a promotional video and caused its parent company, Alphabet, to lose $100 billion in market value (Olson, 2023). That doesn't mean that Bard will be unreliable forever. (It does mean that its marketing team should have been more careful, though...)

The second: After the infancy of an AI tool, accuracy is something to be monitored. After it has been trained, is it improving? When it reaches a level of maturity, is it as accurate as we expect it to be? The longer it has been trained, the smarter it should become. If it isn't getting more intelligent and more accurate, that's cause for concern.

WHAT'S THE IMPACT ON EQUITY?

One of the first very public cases of a schools blocking AI chatbot ChatGPT was New York City Public Schools in January 2023. The district blocked the AI tool for both teachers and students on school computers and networks (Elsen-Rooney, 2023).

One of my first questions was: How will this impact New York City Public School students in the future? Imagine a 10-year-old student in New York City, a fourth grader in the US school system, when that ban was put into place.

What would happen if the ban stayed? That student would spend roughly eight years in NYC schools before graduating high school. In those years, he would have little to no experience or modeling on the appropriate and effective use of AI in the school setting. Imagine the equity gap this would create for this student when he arrived in college. He would be at a competitive disadvantage. Imagine his situation upon college graduation. His lack of experience with the artificial intelligence embedded in his life and work could be a disadvantage in being hired.

Researchers have documented the lack of access to and opportunity in technology for marginalized groups based on gender, race, location, income level, and other factors (Rogers, 2001). These factors could lead to a lack of access to artificial intelligence—its use, its implications, its impact on work—and could create disadvantages, too.

But could it be an equalizer? When students have access to technology—and forward-thinking schools who empower them to learn about AI and its use—they can earn some level of advantage no matter what they look like, where they're born, or how much money their families make.

IF WE USE AI, WHOSE VOICE IS IT REALLY?

I've had some pretty interesting conversations on social media about the implications of AI in teaching and learning.

► One guy told me he never wanted his own children to be taught from lesson plans generated by AI. (Never mind that teachers are completely strapped for time and that we would adjust those plans to best fit our students' needs.)

► Another person asked: What if an AI chatbot writes my emails for me? Is that me? Am I lying when I say I wrote it?

► Yet another pondered: If a teacher generates lesson plans with an AI, who gets the credit? (I wondered what the importance of credit in lesson planning is in the first place, and if creators on Teachers Pay Teachers get credit if a teacher buys lesson plans there.)

At the heart of all of these concerns is one concept: Voice.

It's an important concept, too, and it's a big part of what makes us human. My voice is crucial in my own work. When I taught in the classroom, I spent a lot of time thinking about how I wanted to show up, how I wanted to communicate, and how I wanted students to feel in my class. That's voice. Now, when I write a book or blog post, when I speak in a podcast or a speech or a presentation, even when I create graphics or sketchnotes, I want it to feel uniquely like me.

Our voices are representations of who we are as humans. We want people to know what to expect from us. We want to be authentic.

So, when we use artificial intelligence in our emails, in our teaching, in our planning, in anything, is it authentically us?

To me, I see getting AI assistance like gathering ideas from lots of places. I get ideas when I talk to others, when I watch others teach and speak, and when I read other people's work. I iden-

Our voices are representations of who we are as humans.

tify what I like and discard what I don't. Then I use those ideas as I see fit, and if my use is heavily influenced by someone's idea, I give them credit.

What if my emails are heavily written by an AI assistant? Is that really me? It's an important question you'll have to ponder. To me, if the text the AI generates expresses the idea and sentiment that I want to express, then I adopt its words as mine. In that way, yes, what the AI said is indeed really me. It fits the way I want to show up in the world. If someone asked me if I used AI to create a message I wrote or said, personally, I'd be really transparent about my use of it. But I'd also make clear that the final message it sent—the intent, the tone, the subtext, all of it—was my own responsibility.

This is a question we have to ask to preserve our humanity, and we have to be comfortable with our own answers to this question individually.

WHO WILL IT IMPACT—AND IN WHAT WAYS?

The creative and artistic worlds have voiced concern about AI's impact on their careers and crafts. If AI can create art and poetry and prose, what will it do to people who have spent their lives honing their skills in this area?

Educators have asked these same questions, and I'll bet you've thought about it as well. If artificial intelligence can "teach"—provide answers to questions, guide skill development, provide feedback, and more—what will it do to the careers of skillful, highly qualified educators?

I believe that, as humans, we need to weigh those concerns when we decide if we want to use AI or not for certain tasks. Some things should just be done by humans. We need to decide what those things will be ourselves. When we feel confident in our decisions, we can tell others about how we arrived at them. That will give them more information to make their own decisions.

Of course, all of this will impact our students and their future. If we truly want the best for our students, we'll want to prepare them to thrive in the world they'll live and work in—even if we don't know what that world will look like yet. In the next chapter, we'll discuss steps we can take to help students to be better ready for life in a world with AI integrated throughout.

KEY DEFINITION

TRAINING DATA

The data used to train a machine learning model. The data teaches the AI model how to perform certain tasks. For example, in natural language processing (NLP), which includes many AI assistants, the training data might be lots of text that's been tagged with things like parts of speech, sentiment or tone, and named entities (like people, locations, dates, times, etc.). The larger and more diverse the dataset, the better the model performs. Machine learning models can be trained through interaction with humans, too. Humans can annotate (or tag data) in text or label data in images. Human evaluators assess the output of the machine learning model. Plus, models can learn from interactions with humans when they use the model.

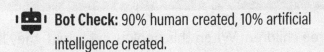 **Bot Check:** 90% human created, 10% artificial intelligence created.

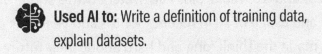 **Used AI to:** Write a definition of training data, explain datasets.

Find a link to the UNESCO recommendations plus shareable infographics at:
AIforEDUbook.com

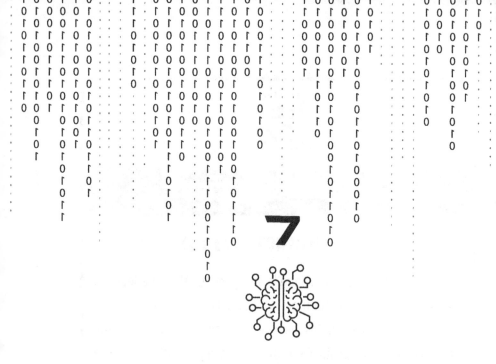

7

PREPARING STUDENTS FOR AN AI-INTEGRATED WORLD

SETTING STUDENTS ON A STRAIGHT PATH TO A FUTURE FULL OF AI

have three children. When this book is published, they'll be 17, 15, and 13 years old. I've watched the surge of discussion and usage of AI in recent months and years. As a dad, it has made me think long and hard about their future. If you are a parent (or act in a similar capacity), I'll bet you've had similar thoughts.

My oldest daughter, Cassie, is a junior in high school. She's going on college visits. As a little girl, she wanted to be a librarian. Later, a coffee shop owner and a pediatric neurosurgeon (maybe at the same time). Then an actor. Right now, she has landed on computer science. With the recent expansion of AI in the world, her future would be really bright on this career track. Cassie gives me hope for an AI-integrated future. If she's helping call the shots, we will all be in good hands.

My youngest daughter, Hallie, is a freshman in high school. She's athletic and smart and witty. She's focused more on living her best life right now and less on choosing a career path (which I respect). It's similar for my son, Joel, a seventh grader. His life revolves around his passions, which include basketball, disc golf, and his family and friends.

Not all of my kids will work in AI. But they'll likely work *with* AI in some capacity. I want to do everything I can to help set them on a path where they'll thrive in their personal and professional lives. They need to know how the growth of AI might impact the career fields they might pursue—and what to do to best position themselves for success.

I'll bet you have similar feelings.

The landscape shifts so quickly. Years ago, I remember education pundits saying that computer programming—writing code—was the path of the future. "Teach students to code above all else!" they said. Now, AI assistants can write code, and we're talking about how coders don't have the same level of job security as they had.

What can we do? Here are some steps you can consider that can help your students make smart choices as their paths lead toward the future.

> **Can we detect irresponsible use of AI and enforce it effectively? Maybe. Maybe not. But we can help students see the impact of their actions.**

DISCUSS RESPONSIBLE USE OF AI.

We've talked a lot about cheating concerns with AI assistants. The core concern is that students won't think, learn, develop necessary skills, or be prepared for the future if AI does all of their work for them.

Can we detect irresponsible use of AI and enforce it effectively? Maybe. Maybe not. But we can help students see the impact of their actions. We can help them learn how AI can be used appropriately and effectively in their work and their personal lives.

When students use AI too heavily for classwork, we can ask:

- ► How do I know what you've learned?
- ► Are there barriers preventing you from doing the work yourself?
- ► Are there ways you could have used AI that would have helped you grow academically and do your best work?

When we notice that someone used AI in problematic ways, we can ask students:

- ► Why do you think this person acted as they did?
- ► What are the benefits and drawbacks of taking that course of action?
- ► How could a situation like this manifest itself in our own lives?
- ► What's a different course of action we could take, and how might it be better?

INTEGRATE MEDIA LITERACY AND DIGITAL CITIZENSHIP.

When artificial intelligence provides an inaccurate, misleading, or biased product, that's **a media literacy issue**. We need to be able to identify, among other things, how valid information is, where it came from, and what influenced the message.

When we use AI-created content inappropriately, that's **a digital citizenship issue**. We need to know, among others, how to show up responsibly in digital spaces, to interact, to represent ourselves and facts accurately, ethically, and responsibly.

Media literacy and digital citizenship aren't just lessons taught by other teachers in other classes. They're fundamental life skills that will serve our students throughout their lives. When everyone understands at least the basics of media literacy and digital citizenship, we can embed those micro conversations in class discussions, in one-on-one conversations with students, and in our lessons in an authentic way.

TEACH STUDENTS TO BECOME GREAT PROMPT ENGINEERS.

Have you ever done a search on a search engine and gotten really poor results? Then, did you add a word or two or rephrase your search query to get exactly what you were looking for?

You were a search engineer. You were creating the best search query possible to get the results you were looking for.

As AI assistants grow in use—and as AI is integrated into many facets of our lives—being a good prompt engineer can serve us well. We might ask an AI assistant to do something and experience it doing a poor job. But if we learn the patterns, the wording, the strategies that create great results from AI, the AI becomes a more valuable tool for us—and we become more valuable because of what we can make it do.

We can help students become great prompt engineers by studying what makes effective AI prompts and sharing that with them. We can also help students reflect on prompts they've created to see what was effective, what wasn't, and whether successful changes they made could help them create better prompts in the future.

Plus, if they get good at it, being a prompt engineer could lead to a lucrative career (Harwell, 2023).

EMPHASIZE THE IMPORTANCE OF TAKING ACTION.

The results given to us by artificial intelligence tools can only take us so far. The vision of what to do with them—and the execution of that vision—are still attributes that make us special as humans.

This reminds me of the movie *Hidden Figures*. Of course, these women of color inspired us with their excellence and perseverance to forge past race and gender barriers. But their story also can give us hope as we learn about the place of artificial intelligence in education.

NASA's efforts to win the space race were dependent upon the skills of these women, called "human computers." They did advanced mathematical calculations by hand. Their accuracy was crucial to the success of NASA's Apollo missions. Eventually, NASA started transitioning these calculations to machines—IBM computers—which would eventually render these women's human work obsolete.

Ideas are nothing without vision and execution.

As artificial intelligence grows exponentially, pundits and gurus announce the end of careers and the obsolescence of certain skills. When these IBM computers came to NASA, did anyone decry this as the end of NASA? Absolutely not. These machines helped NASA's engineers to do their work more efficiently, allowing them to do more in less time. The computers. Humans still had to execute on the calculations. Humans still had to dream, to envision what could be done beyond the confines of our own planet. Machines didn't render NASA obsolete; they made NASA more agile.

And, in the end, it was NASA supervisor Dorothy Vaughan who realized that this new technology wasn't the downfall of her team of human computers. It was job security. Without access to manuals or formal training, Vaughan learned the basics of Fortran and trained her colleagues on it.

The proliferation of AI doesn't mean we don't need humans anymore. AI can do the basics for us so we can spend more time on higher-level tasks, planning, and realizing our vision.

Ideas are nothing without vision and execution.

RECOGNIZE THE SPECIAL VALUE OF OUR HUMANITY.

Sherry Turkle has studied our relationship with technology for decades. In her research, as she described in her TED Talk (2012), she studied the use of robotic pets in nursing homes. These robot companions, in the shape of a dog or a seal, would appear to listen to elderly patients, respond, and comfort them when they may be alone otherwise.

The first time I watched this TED Talk, initially, I thought this sounded great. These people had companionship in the isolation of a nursing home.

Sherry's reaction was the polar opposite. She said: "As that woman took comfort in her robot companion, I didn't find it amazing; I found it one of the most wrenching, complicated moments in my 15 years of work. But when I stepped back, I felt myself at the cold, hard center of a perfect storm. *We expect more from technology and less from each other.* And I ask myself, 'Why have things come to this?'"

Wow. We expect more from technology and less from fellow humans.

What does it mean to be a person? What makes us special as human beings?

A crucial question we must confront in the face of this influx of artificial intelligence is this: What does it mean to be a person? What makes us special as human beings? What can we do that artificial intelligence can't—or what are we better at? These are crucial questions that students will have to reckon with immediately and in the future. Even if we don't have answers to those questions, we can participate in conversations about them.

Let's keep asking: how do we leverage our most precious asset: our humanity?

KEY DEFINITION

NATURAL LANGUAGE PROCESSING (NLP)

Focuses on the interactions between humans and computers in natural language. When NLP is done well, it helps computers understand language, interpret it, and create language that's meaningful and useful to humans. NLP can be used in language translation. It can also be used in sentiment analysis to determine the tone of a passage of text.

 Bot Check: 85% human created, 15% artificial intelligence created.

 Used AI to: Write a definition of natural language processing, provide details from the true story of the movie *Hidden Figures*.

Find bonus resources, shareable infographics, and more at:
AIforEDUbook.com

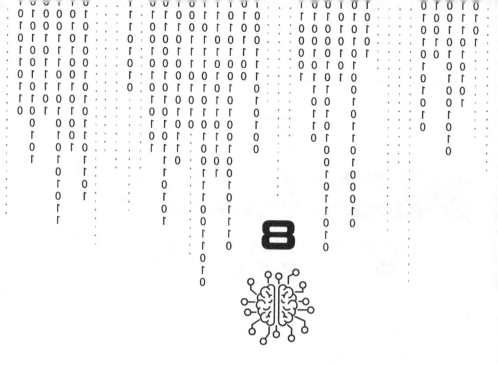

8

TAKING BOLD STEPS
TOWARD THE FUTURE

We pictured the AI world from the movies at the beginning of this book. It might not be too far off in some ways.

- ► We might not have Rosey the Robot from *The Jetsons*, but we do have robot vacuums that clean the floor while we're away.
- ► We might not have HAL 9000 from *2001: A Space Odyssey*, but we do have assistants like Siri, Alexa, and Google to perform simple tasks.
- ► Cafe 80s from *Back to the Future: Part II* might not exist, but we can order food digitally at a kiosk at McDonald's without a human cashier.

What's it going to look like as AI develops and assimilates itself into our lives? We're starting to get glimpses, but it's still pretty unclear.

What our students really need is one thing: Imperfect answers. When we don't have clear answers, imperfect answers empower us to move forward.

Our students need teachers who are willing to consider how their future will differ from ours and bravely explore this new frontier with them. (And they need school leaders, lawmakers, parents, and community members who will give space, grace, and encouragement to make this happen.)

> **When we don't have clear answers, imperfect answers empower us to move forward.**

Our students don't need clairvoyant teachers with an exact vision of the future to perfectly position them for success. What they need are teachers who are open and aware. Who are curious. Who are willing to experiment and get it wrong sometimes in hopes that, eventually, with enough trial and error and learning, they'll get it right.

Imperfect answers are better than no answers. They're better than the status quo.

Imperfect answers are our only hope of getting something resembling perfect answers—and getting them in a timely enough fashion to prepare students for success. Here are a few things to keep in mind as you seek out your imperfect answers:

DON'T FORGET YOUR "TOMORROW GLASSES."

We remember how we were taught as students. We remember how we have taught in the classroom recently. (Some of us remember teaching in the very distant past!) Those memories use "today glasses." Right now, we need "tomorrow glasses."

Using "tomorrow glasses" is based more on anticipation and learning, less on past experience. AI isn't going to change *everything*. Many of the tenets of sound pedagogy don't change. How we apply them, though, might. Plan instruction with this question front and center: "Does this prepare my students for *their* futures?"

REMEMBER THAT AI IS FOR YOU, TOO.

I believe that time is the most precious currency for teachers. If we're going to do our best work, support our students, and fulfill our teaching dreams, more time will help us realize that dream faster and better. AI can give us time. And we're really, really good at investing that time in ways that will pay dividends for our students.

AI can't teach the way you do. But it can give you lesson plan ideas. It can give you practice questions and discussion prompts. It can offer feedback on your students' work. It's up to you whether you use any content it creates for you and in what ways.

If we're going to do our best work, support our students, and fulfill our teaching dreams, more time will help us realize that dream faster and better. AI can give us time.

In the end, if using AI tools cuts your planning time from 30 minutes to 18 minutes—or your grading time from 40 minutes to 22—that extra time it creates is yours. Use it however you wish. Plan out that cool lesson you've always wanted to do. Or go home early. The choice is yours. I know this type of decision feels pretty foreign to us—deciding what to do with extra time. Whether we use it to do something amazing for our students or preserve our mental health, everyone wins.

KEEP A HEALTHY BLEND OF OPTIMISM AND SKEPTICISM.

AI isn't going to save the world. But it isn't going to ruin it, either. So far, no innovation in the history of the world has been able to ruin everything. The same is true for education. It has the potential for harm if we're not careful, and it has the potential for greatness if applied properly.

Try to avoid all-or-nothing thinking. Keeping an open mind prevents you from blocking out a viable option for your students and yourself.

SOLID LEARNING IS STILL THE CORE OF WHAT WE DO.

As long as technology has been a part of the classroom, this maxim has been true: great teaching is fundamental. Technology can't make poor teaching good. Solid teaching, however, can overcome just about anything. If you're optimistic about AI (like me), beware not to forsake quality teaching and learning to force it. But be sure to tell your inner skeptic to be willing to try. That teaching idea that might have some flaws immediately might lead to something meaningful in the future.

HAVE CONVERSATIONS.

Talk about all of this: the concerns, the fears, the possibilities, the implementation, even your emotions around it. Talk to your colleagues. Talk to your students. Talk to your school leaders. Talk to people in your community. If given the chance, talk to people who work in AI and computer science. Have conversations, even if you don't fully understand what you're talking about. More perspectives help get you closer to reality, and you might learn something.

IT'S NO LONGER SCIENCE FICTION. AI IS HERE.

Like the anonymous reader in my survey said, "It's unavoidable, whether I'm excited or not." It's here, and it can do way more than write asparagus rap lyrics and apocalyptic stories about pop culture icons.

It's our students' future. And it's our future, too. Whether we're excited or not. The fact that you made it to the end of the book shows something that should make us all optimistic about education: you're open-minded, and you want to learn about it.

AI will change constantly. That doesn't mean you have to be on the cutting, bleeding edge. A little understanding and a lot of application will take you far.

And stay connected. We at Ditch That Textbook are committed to keeping you informed and sharing ideas for your classroom. If you haven't joined our mailing list, go to DitchThatTextbook.com/join to keep a steady pipeline of ideas in your inbox.

Learn. Explore. Ponder. Discuss. Try. Test. Reflect.

Your students will thank you.

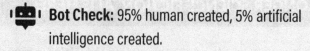
Find bonus resources, shareable infographics, and more at:

AIforEDUbook.com

ABOUT THE AUTHOR

Matt Miller taught in public schools for more than 10 years, teaching all levels of high school Spanish. In his career, he planned nearly 12,000 class lessons. He taught more than half a million instructional minutes. And he graded work for nearly 2,000 days of class. He was recognized for classroom excellence with the WTHI-TV Golden Apple Award and as a two-time nominee for the Bammy! Awards Secondary Teacher of the Year.

He's the author of six books: *Ditch That Textbook, Ditch That Homework, Don't Ditch That Tech, Tech Like A PIRATE, Do More With Google Classroom*, and *AI for Educators*. He is a Google Certified Innovator and the co-host of the Digital Learning Podcast. He holds a Master of Education in curriculum and instruction from Indiana State University.

He lives in west central Indiana and says that he's living the dream: happily married with three kids, three dogs, and a massive cell phone bill.

SPEAKING

Matt Miller is a sought-after speaker in K-12 education, having presented in-person or virtually at more than 300 events in six countries and 45 states (plus the Northern Mariana Islands).

His **keynote speeches** are a skillful mix of humor, storytelling, practical ideas, and empowerment. With a decade of classroom teaching experience, Matt relates to teachers— and also inspires them with new ideas and perspectives. He trained at Heroic Public Speaking GRAD, the most substantial and complete speaker training in the world.

His **workshops** are engaging, practical, and hands-on. Teachers use new ideas in class the next day. They come away infused with pedagogy, brain science, technology, and inspiration, going beyond the passive "check out this cool website" style of training.

Matt's **"AI for Educators" sessions** have been well-attended at conferences, filling rooms and prompting conference organizers to book additional sessions. They're full of practical ideas, questions to consider, and practices to emulate, giving teachers a tangible path forward.

For more information, availability, and pricing, email **hello@ DitchThatTextbook.com**.

REFERENCES

Brockman, G. [@gdb]. (2022, Dec. 5). *ChatGPT just crossed 1 million users; it's been 5 days since launch* [Tweet]. Twitter. https://twitter.com/gdb/status/1599683104142430208

Cornell Law School. (n.d.). *Intellectual property.* Legal Information Institute. Retrieved February 27, 2023, from https://www.law.cornell.edu/wex/intellectual_property

Elsen-Rooney, M. (2023, January 3). *NYC Education Department blocks CHATGPT on school devices, networks.* Chalkbeat New York. Retrieved February 27, 2023, from https://ny.chalkbeat.org/2023/1/3/23537987/nyc-schools-ban-chatgpt-writing-artificial-intelligence

Gartner. (2022, May 17). *Gartner Hype Cycle research methodology.* Gartner. Retrieved February 27, 2023, from https://www.gartner.com/en/research/methodologies/gartner-hype-cycle

Harwell, D. (2023, February 25). Tech's hottest new job: AI whisperer. No coding required. *The Washington Post.* Retrieved February 27, 2023, from https://www.washingtonpost.com/technology/2023/02/25/prompt-engineers-techs-next-big-job/

Herman, D. (2022, December 16). *The end of high-school English.* The Atlantic. Retrieved February 27, 2023, from https://www.theatlantic.com/technology/archive/2022/12/openai-chatgpt-writing-high-school-english-essay/672412/

Hu, K. (2023, February 2). *ChatGPT sets record for fastest-growing user base - analyst note.* Reuters. Retrieved February 27, 2023, from https://www.reuters.com/technology/chatgpt-sets-record-fastest-growing-user-base-analyst-note-2023-02-01/

Lee, K.-F. (2022, March 16). *How AI will completely change the way we live in the next 20 years.* Medium. Retrieved February 27, 2023, from https://kaifulee.medium.com/how-ai-will-completely-change-the-way-we-live-in-the-next-20-years-e27a855b1bd0

Levin, J. R. (1988). *Elaboration-based learning strategies: Powerful theory= powerful application.* Contemporary Educational Psychology, 13(3), 191-205.

Loizos, C. [Connie Loizos]. (2023, January 17). *StrictlyVC in conversation with Sam Altman, part two (OpenAI)* [Video]. YouTube. https://www.youtube.com/watch?v=ebjkD1Om4uw

Marche, S. (2022, December 16). *The college essay is dead.* The Atlantic. Retrieved February 27, 2023, from https://www.theatlantic.com/technology/archive/2022/12/chatgpt-ai-writing-college-student-essays/672371/

Miller, M. [Ditch That Textbook]. (2023, February 22). *Navigating ChatGPT, chatbots, and artificial intelligence in education (panel discussion)* [Video]. YouTube. https://www.youtube.com/watch?v=1-X4d2Nbgtw

Olson, E. (2023, February 9). *Google shares drop $100 billion after its new AI chatbot makes a mistake.* NPR. Retrieved February 27, 2023, from https://www.npr.org/2023/02/09/1155650909/google-chatbot-error-bard-shares

Rogers, E. M. (2001). The digital divide. *Convergence: The International Journal of Research into New Media Technologies,* 7(4), 96–111. https://doi.org/10.1177/135485650100700406

Turkle, S. (2012). *Connected, but alone?* [Video]. TED Conferences. https://www.ted.com/talks/sherry_turkle_connected_but_alone

United Nations Educational, Scientific and Cultural Organization. (2022, November 23). *Recommendation on the ethics of artificial intelligence* (Programme Document SHS/BIO/PI/2021/1). Retrieved from the United Nations Educational, Scientific and Cultural Organization website: https://unesdoc.unesco.org/ark:/48223/pf0000381137